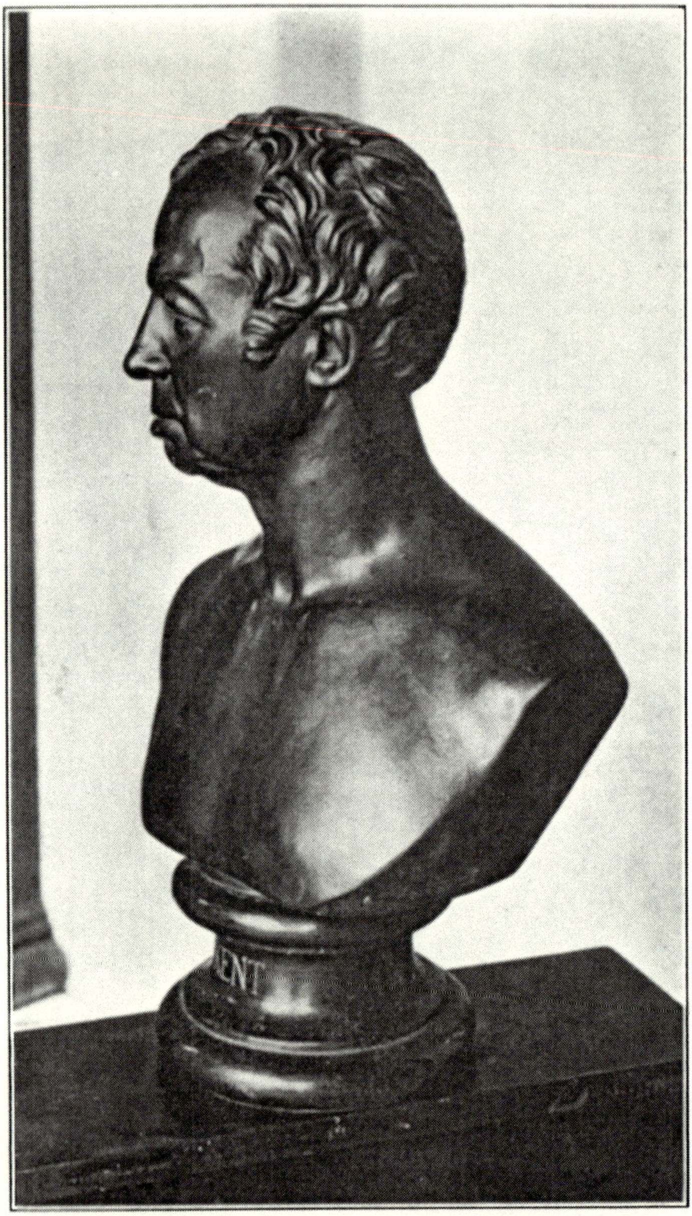

Chancellor James Kent

MEN AND BOOKS FAMOUS IN THE LAW

BY

FREDERICK C. HICKS, A.M., LL.B.

Associate Professor of Legal Bibliography, and Law Librarian
Columbia University Law School

WITH AN INTRODUCTION

BY

HARLAN F. STONE

Dean, Columbia University Law School

THE LAWBOOK EXCHANGE, LTD.

Clark, New Jersey

2008

ISBN-13: 978-0-9630106-2-9 (cloth)
ISBN-10: 0-9630106-2-X (cloth)
ISBN-13: 978-1-58477-919-3 (paperback)
ISBN-10: 1-58477-919-5 (paperback)

The quality of this reprint is equivalent to the quality of the original work.

THE LAWBOOK EXCHANGE, LTD.
33 Terminal Avenue
Clark, New Jersey 07066-1321

Please see our website for a selection of our other publications and fine facsimile reprints of classic works of legal history:
www.lawbookexchange.com

Library of Congress Cataloging-in-Publication Data

Hicks, Frederick C. (Frederick Charles), b. 1875.
Men and books famous in the law / by Frederick C. Hicks ; with an introduction by Harlan F. Stone.
259 p. : ill. ; 22 cm.
ISBN: 096301062X
Originally published: Rochester, N.Y. : Lawyers Co-operative Pub. Co., 1921.
Includes bibliographical references (p. 237-245) and index.
Lawyers—United States. Lawyers—Great Britain. Law—Bibliography.
KF353 .H5 1992
349.73/0922 B 347.300922 B 20

Printed in the United States of America on acid-free paper

MEN AND BOOKS FAMOUS IN THE LAW

BY

FREDERICK C. HICKS, A.M., LL.B.

Associate Professor of Legal Bibliography, and Law Librarian
Columbia University Law School

WITH AN INTRODUCTION

BY

HARLAN F. STONE

Dean, Columbia University Law School

ROCHESTER, NEW YORK

THE LAWYERS CO-OPERATIVE PUBLISHING CO.

1921

E. R. ANDREWS PRINTING COMPANY, Rochester, N. Y.

TO

NATHAN ABBOTT

Whose Interest and Encouragement Have Made
This Work Possible

CONTENTS

ILLUSTRATIONS

PREFACE

The following sketches have been drawn as illustrations of the appeal which law books have when considered as the product of human needs, experience and environment. Out of the hundreds of authors and books that might have been considered, the selection of these few has been made almost at random—because they happened to be of special interest to the author. Nevertheless, it will be found that most of the great classes of law books are discussed or referred to, as well as the problems that have arisen in the progress of law-book publication. Statute law is represented by Livingston's Code; law reports by those of Blackstone, Coke, Dyer, Peters, Plowden and Wheaton; digests by Viner's Abridgment; dictionaries by Cowell's Interpreter; institutional works by Coke, Cowell, Blackstone and Kent; monographs by those of Littleton and Wheaton.

These studies deal only with Anglo-American law books. They are the outgrowth of lectures and seminar work given by the author in the Columbia University Law School, in a course on Legal Bibliography, and lectures to students in Library Economy in several Library Schools.

No pretense is made of giving an adequate picture of the contents of the books. That would require a technical presentation which would defeat the end sought. Nor is a complete picture of the authors of the books given. The studies are merely impressionistic sketches of men and books famous in the law, with glimpses here and there of the events and people of the time in which the books were written, published and read. The last word is not said on any of the men and books treated. To some readers unacquainted with the law, this book will be the first word on the subject; to others it will be only a reminder of things already known; and to others it will supply details on matters already generally understood. To all, it is hoped that the book will give some inspiration to look further in the realms of legal literature.

Grateful acknowledgment is made to Professors John Bassett Moore, Nathan Abbott and Henry F. Munro for reading portions of the manuscript, and to Dean Harlan F. Stone, for reading all of it.

FREDERICK C. HICKS.

Columbia University,
May 11, 1921.

INTRODUCTION

By Harlan F. Stone

The development of law study in the United States since 1870 constitutes a remarkable chapter in the history of education. When in 1794 Kent, who stands out as in many respects the most gifted and attractive figure in the annals of American jurisprudence, began his law lectures in Columbia College, they were attended by "seven students and thirty-six gentlemen, chiefly lawyers and law students who did not belong to the college." Three years later he abandoned his professorship for want of students. When in 1823, after a distinguished judicial career during which he had achieved a national reputation as a liberal scholar and jurist, he returned to his professorship, the maximum attendance at his lectures was "thirty-three gentlemen and fourteen private students." Even in the heyday of the Dane Law School, later the Harvard Law School, under the leadership of Parker, Parsons, and Washburn, that school had little to identify it, either in methods of work or in the number of its students, with our modern system of legal education wherein numerous schools scattered throughout the country are thronged with eager students who devote three and often more years to the purely academic study of their chosen profession.

It is not the purpose of this brief introduction to inquire into the causes for this surprising development. They have been too often and too thoroughly discussed to require any elucidation here. It will suffice if the attention be directed to certain outstanding characteristics of the new order which make the production of this little volume by Professor Hicks an extremely interesting and valuable experiment.

With the very general adoption of the case method of instruction in American law schools, the day of law study from institutes and authoritative treatises as original sources was at an end. For nearly a generation now, law study in all the important centers of legal learning has been dominated by the scientific spirit which rejects the dogmatic statement of legal doctrine and demands that every legal principle be traced to its original source in judicial precedent, and be re-examined in the light of its relation to social utility. The new order began with the insistence upon the study of precedent as the original and practically the only source of legal knowledge; but it did not stop there. In our own time there has been a growing recognition of the fact that precedents cannot be justly valued and intelligently applied without some adequate understanding of the social and economic conditions out of which they sprang and to which in our own day they must be applied; and of late there has been a marked tendency toward a more searching analysis of the fundamental concepts on the basis of which our legal structure is reared, and greater emphasis upon a more precise and exact use of legal terminology. These are all manifestations of the scientific spirit which in every field of human endeavor is giving us more exact knowledge and increased capacity for its utilization.

In such a scheme of things there is small scope for the authoritative pronouncements of any individual, however penetrating his intellect and however gifted he may be in his powers of expression. It rejects the pedantry of Coke, it sets little store by the artificial reasoning of Blackstone, and it prefers the opinions of Kent the judge and the chancellor to the mellifluous passages of Kent the commentator. It is not surprising therefore that the figures of the great lawyers and commentators treated of in this volume, so vivid and outstanding to law students of an earlier day, are becoming shadowy and indistinct to the students and the lawyers of this generation. In this interesting and valuable series of studies Professor Hicks challenges the attention with the query whether we have done well to let them become so.

That, by the application of scientific methods to law study, legal knowledge and juristic science have been the gainers, no one familiar with the work carried on in the great centers of legal study in this country can doubt. How great the gain is no one can now say. At least another generation must pass before we can begin to gather its fruits in abundance and to form some estimate of what we may hope to be accomplished by it. But this great gain has not been without some attendant loss. The modern law student has gained in the exactness of his legal knowledge, in his familiarity with the history of legal doctrine, and above all in his power of analysis and his capacity to apply legal principles to new states of fact. But he is the loser in his lack of intimate contact with the precision and thoroughness of Littleton and Coke, with the literary style of Blackstone, and the liberal and enlightened spirit of Kent. In our passion for science we have been prone to overlook the human element in the development of law.

After all, law is the product of human experience. Into its warp and woof have entered human interests, human needs, human emotions, and notions of ethics and philosophy which are the product of our racial experience.

At intervals during the eight or nine centuries since the Common Law began to take form, there have appeared the figures of the great commentators. One can almost count them on the fingers of one hand—Bracton, Glanville, Littleton, Coke, Blackstone and Kent. They and some others of lesser note have definitely and visibly influenced the development of our law. What that influence has been, what manner of men they were, how their work was done, and what were the vicissitudes of their publications in those centuries are questions of vital interest to every lawyer and student of the law, and the answer to them is of positive educational value. Without abatement of the scientific spirit, we can do much to humanize law and law study. We can no longer study Coke and Blackstone and Kent as the very foundation stones of the law; but we can glean much from their lives and work and from the lives and work of those who, like them, have permanently influenced legal thought, to give to law study its human interest and to increase its real value. This the author has done; and in doing it has rendered a service to every earnest student of the law, who will find in his pages inspiration to know more of the makers of the great law books.

Of especial interest to American law students are the author's accounts of Livingston and Wheaton. They did not affect the current of legal thinking in the same manner or to the same extent as did Kent, or indeed any of the other subjects of these essays, but Wheaton gave the first great impetus to the study of international law in this country. His writings have been widely read abroad and have exercised a potent influence there.

Livingston, whose life, judged by the immediate results of his work, has been counted as almost a failure, united in his extraordinary mentality legal knowledge, practical idealism and a unique capacity to give concrete expression to it in legislation which gave him a positive genius for codification. He was fully a century in advance of the legal thought of his time, but as the problems of law improvement through legislation and codification press more and more upon us we shall turn more often to his life and work for guidance and inspiration. The lives of both men are replete with human and dramatic interest. They are interwoven with our legal history and touch at innumerable points the lives of those famous in the chronicles of our law.

One could wish that other masters of legal literature had been included in the list selected by the author, and express the hope that the success of this volume may encourage the production of a second in which they may be included.

MEN AND BOOKS FAMOUS IN THE LAW

CHAPTER I

The Human Appeal of Law Books

To transmute base metals into fine gold, to reconcile the irreconcilable, these are vain attempts. Why then seek elements of human appeal in law books? Is there any such thing? The majority of people would answer at once that the question contains a contradiction in terms. As well suppose that there is human interest in a treatise on differential calculus as in a law book! It is true that to those who know the story of the development of mathematical science and its connection with the progress of civilization, even calculus has an appeal all its own; but to the general reader, the proposition is not self-evident. Neither is it self-evident that law books have any interest that is not purely utilitarian. When seen in a lawyer's office, or on the shelves of a great library, law books appear to be only the uninteresting tools of a trade. They lack that diversity of form which attracts the eye and arouses the curiosity. There they stand, row after row, uniform in binding, in color, and in size, distinguishable from each other only by different stages of dilapidation and decay. And if the layman has the hardihood to look into these books on pleasure bent, and not in pursuit of necessary information, is any better impression given? Perhaps he has selected one of the Year Books (the earliest English reports of law cases) and he finds that it is written in a mongrel kind of French, and printed in a type that confuses the eye. Or he has hit upon some modern law report containing the opinions of judges who delight in technical terms and use an involved style which repels the intellect. Or he attempts to read a statute, and finds that in construction it rivals the intricacies of the longest German sentences, and in the profuse use of synonyms puts Walt Whitman to shame, while wholly lacking his imagery. Or he takes down a ponderous digest, which is apparently made up of a hodge podge of unrelated paragraphs, grouped under mysterious headings, and ornamented with hieroglyphics of combined letters and figures. Or he has in hand a treatise, the title of which conveys no meaning to him and the contents of which seem to defy comprehension. So far, it must be admitted that law books are forbidding, in whatever superficial way we look at them. They do not have the attraction of a brightly jacketed novel, nor are they "easy reading" to the uninitiated.

Granting all this, it does not follow that, to the discerning reader, law books are devoid of human appeal. Overcome the natural repugnance of the layman to law books, examine them at first hand, think of their authors as living men, give even so brief attention to technical terms as is required of the operator of an automobile, and law books take on a new aspect.

Law books have a human appeal because of what they contain, and what they represent in the history of society; because of their place in English literature; because they are impressive historical and biographical documents; and because of the vicissitudes through which some of the great books have passed.

The Contents of Law Books

A distinguishing characteristic of law is its universality. Avoid the law as we will, it nevertheless creeps into the language and thought of our daily lives, and becomes part of our domestic, social and political environment. Throughout the ages, it has been a progressive, mobile thing, the result and expression of civilization rather than its source. Law is not divorced from life; it is an intimate part of it. Law is a subject which in every era forms an essential stratum in the structure of society. Cleave down through any part of this structure, seeking the foundations upon which modern philosophy, religion, history, economics, and sociology are built, and you come to a layer of law—not lawyer's law alone, but the people's law,—law which is the product of human experience. That there is a legal side to nearly every subject of investigation and research is a conclusion that cannot be escaped.

And so, law books, which are the tangible evidences of what the law is, can no more be set aside as things remote from life, than can the law itself. They are not merely technical books which have application only to a special science of restricted scope; but they have played and continue to play a part in the development of the enduring things of life,—philosophy, religion, social concepts, justice, humanitarian interest, political organization. They record history in its most authentic form. In the statute books are laid down rules for the benefit of all in the preservation of rights, the punishment and correction of wrongs, and the administration of government. The great charters are beacon lights of human progress. In law reports are the conclusions reached by judges in actual controversies between living persons.

Motives are shown. Error, enmity, weakness, cupidity, crime are there; but also purity, openness, goodwill and strength of purpose. Life is there with the gloss rubbed off;—tragedy, comedy, sordidness, meanness, manners, customs, superstition, tradition. All are truly pictured here by contemporary evidence. Back of the arguments of contending counsel, back of the opinions and decisions of the judges, is always some story of human interest. It may be only the sordid story of a mismated husband and wife, or of a trivial neighborhood quarrel; but it may be the epic of "big business," or of the tragedy of treason, or of the heroism of a prize crew in a captured vessel. In treatises and commentaries, we find reasoned statements of the law under which men live, discussion of legal concepts of human significance and philosophical import, reflecting the best thought of the time in which they were written, and sometimes filled with the personality of their authors.

Law Books as Literature

That law books as a class are not *belles-lettres* may be taken for granted. As we know them to-day their chief characteristics are not beauty of thought or elegance of style, but accuracy and clarity of statement often at the expense of style. Yet law and the politer forms of literature are in their origins closely akin. Before the use of writing, the poet, lawyer and historian were one. It was by act of memory, and by constant repetition, that the story of battles, of unusual events, and the record of customs were handed down from generation to generation. To assist the memory, says Jeudwine (The Manufacture of Historical Material, p. 14), "the help of rhythm, of musical sound, of polished verse, was called in, in all the literatures of all the nations of which we have knowledge, to make endure in the mind of the bard the doubtful wanderings of the law, the uncertain event of the battle, the remote birth and origin of the race." Thus the poet, lawyer and historian were combined, and the poet, by the very act of putting customary laws into verse for the purpose of preserving them, was an interpreter and often a creator of law. The poetic character of early oral versifications of law has survived the advent of printing, and we find that many charters, famous statutes, forms of pleading and judicial oaths in use to-day in the courts of law, flow from the tongue in poetic metre. They have the same musical quality and rhythmical cadence as have chants and responses in the English prayer book. A serious attempt to use rhythm and rhyme to assist the memory and emphasize the chief points of law is found in the "Reports of Sir Edward Coke, Kt. in Verse," published in 1742, in which each case in eleven volumes of his Reports is put into a couplet.

The language and style of the great English law books, while affected by the technical character of their subject-matter, and by the development of law as a profession, are no more complex and disconcerting than the language and style of theology, philosophy or ethics. The books take their characteristics from the period in which they were written. For example, in the statutes, reports, and treatises of Elizabeth's reign, we have the prose of writers contemporaneous with Shakespeare. The law books of the next reign are in the style of the King James version of the Bible. The involved, fulsome, florid style of Coke was not his creation, but was in common use by the learned.[1]

[1] See Beer, Thomas: Coke Literature, Ohio State Bar Association, 30: 182–206.

Conceiving of literature as made up of books which "are marked by elevation, vigor, and catholicity of thought, by fitness, purity, and grace of style, and by artistic construction," many of the great law books in every period since the beginning of law printing are found to come within this definition. They possess much more than mere accuracy and clarity. Their style and rhetorical construction are influenced by the nobility, dignity, and rugged originality of their subject-matter. Examples of legal writings of high literary quality may be found in forensic oratory, and many judicial opinions are without doubt works of literature. They have breadth of view, vision, sympathy, and lofty perception, expressed in a pure and facile style. The prefaces of law books,—reports, treatises, digests,—are often fine examples of the art of the essayist. The Bills of Rights in written constitutions embody noble concepts in noble language. The preambles of the early American and English statutes, though sometimes fulsome, are yet fine products of moral, religious and patriotic thought. The Commentaries by Blackstone and Kent, and the monographs by Bigelow, Holmes, Robinson, Odgers and Sugden, are the work of masters of English style.

Law Books as Historical and Biographical Documents

One of the mistakes of those who have not cultivated an acquaintance with law books is to assume that they are products of the labors of extraordinary persons who have little in common with the rest of humanity. How absurd this is, is seen as soon as we admit the universal application of the law, the consequent scope of law books, and the many attributes of literature which they possess.

How comes it that such books have been written, if there are not great personalities back of them? Not negligible as persons are those who have drafted the great charters and statutes; who in great judicial causes have written epoch making opinions and reached enduring decisions; who have composed with creative genius the classical treatises of the law. Nor were they mere clerks who compiled the great law dictionaries, abridgments and digests based on the source-books of the law. Even those men were notable in their times, some of them judges and dignitaries of state. And so it is that if we inquire when, where, and by whom, the great English and American law books were produced, we find ourselves in the realm of history and biography. For instance, to provide a historical setting for the books whose story is told in the subsequent chapters, it has been necessary to range superficially through a period of more than 450 years, from 1422, when Littleton was born, to 1881, when ended the great suit of Lawrence v. Dana. The story of Littleton begins in a tiny village in the England of the Wars of the Roses. It is not yet ended. Coke and Cowell draw us into the London era of Elizabeth, James I., Charles I. and the Protectorate. They were contemporaries and associates of a group of men and women whose names are by-words of history, literature, politics and religion,—Shakespeare, Marlowe, Bacon, Archbishops Bancroft and Laud, and the Duke of Buckingham. Cowell was a representative of the Civil and Ecclesiastical Law, and held a chair at Cambridge. In the combined story of Cowell, Coke and Bacon we come into contact with two great legal controversies—that between the Church and the Common Law, and that between the latter and the Courts of Chancery. In the political arena, they illustrate the contest between the Crown, with its prerogatives, and the House of Commons. With Blackstone we visit Oxford, see a picture of academic life in the early years of the eighteenth century, and learn how University teaching of the Common Law in England began. The influence of Blackstone reached across the Atlantic, and his work was taken up by James Kent. In following his career, and that of Livingston, we learn something of Revolutionary days in the Colonies, of interruption to the education of college students by the advent of war, of readjustment when war had ended, of the creation and development of the United States as a sovereign state, of the development of courts of law and of equity in this country, of politics and the play of personal forces. Blackstone's Commentaries are the product of Oxford lectures; Kent's are the product of legal teaching in the early days of Columbia University. In his own account of these lectures and the books which grew out of them, we have a first-hand view of college life in America before 1830. Livingston and Wheaton were contemporaries of Kent, and all three were associates of Hamilton, Adams, Jefferson, Webster, Jackson and the other great figures of the time. Livingston's story includes life in New York City, in New Orleans just after the Louisiana Purchase, in Washington, and in the court of France during the time of Louis Philippe. Livingston's great controversy with Jefferson over the Batture lands produced classic examples of controversial literature, which in spite of the bitterness of the parties are models of learning, argument and deduction. And throughout his life he was possessed of a great purpose to reform the system of criminal law in the United States. His purpose found expression in a work the influence of which spread to the whole world. Henry Wheaton, a student, lawyer, writer and diplomat, leads us, in the events of his life, from Providence to New York, thence to Washington, thence to Copenhagen and to Berlin. The story of his books is the story of his daily life in the realms of literature, history, and private and public law. His United States Supreme Court Reports form a chapter not only in his own life but in that of a great body of Federal judges during the formative period of the United States government. His great work on international law was the subject of a bitter personal quarrel and legal battle between two men famous in their own right in American annals, William Beach Lawrence and Richard Henry Dana.

Great law books are so much a part of the social fabric of their times that they are in themselves historical documents. They are as truly biographical documents in the lives of their authors, most of whom are men of note quite aside from their fame as law writers. Easily obtained evidence leads to the conclusion that these men were not "mere lawyers," and that the human side of their characters was developed to an unusual degree by contact with life in all of its kaleidoscopic aspects. And while they influenced the world through their books, their own lives were often very much affected by them. For instance, Cowell's life was ruined by his dictionary; Coke lost his Chief-Justiceship partly on account of his law reports; Blackstone would probably have been a mediocre practicing attorney to the end of his days had he not had the impetus to lecture and to write. He became a judge on the strength of the reputation derived from his Commentaries. Kent changed the *decrescendo* of forced retirement from the chancellorship of New York, into a *crescendo,* in the waning years of his life, by writing his Commentaries. Livingston preserved himself from despair and the evil effects of rancor in the face of financial disaster and a generation's unsuccessful struggle with fortune, by the pursuit of an ideal. While he succeeded eventually as a lawyer, statesman, and diplomat, it was his Louisiana Penal Code, the expression of a humanitarian ideal, which made his success something more than a personal victory.

The Story of the Books Themselves

If, in the following chapters, the error is made of bestowing fulsome praise upon the men about whose books the sketches are written, it is because the initial appeal grows as one studies their work, and realizes that these men wrote, hampered by all those human limitations which most of us use as excuses for lack of accomplishment. With two exceptions, the books were written while their authors were under the stress of other labors. Bibliography would be a dry and uncongenial task if it were not for biography. Bibliography, in its present meaning, is the systematic description of books with special reference to their authorship, titles, publishers, dates, history, editions, subject-matter and value either material or intellectual. A list of books, however great they may be, however many editions they have run to, and however accurately they may be described, makes no very readable page. But biography adds the leaven of sympathy which lightens for the book-lover the sad loaf of bibliography. Some books there are, however, which have romantic stories of their own, have passed through unusual vicissitudes, and have survived disaster. The life of these cannot be shown by annotated lists, but must be told in connected narratives, which bridge the gaps between successive editions. It was not mere chance that made it a tradition in the Inns of Court to read Littleton's Tenures completely through each Christmas day, just as many read Dickens' Christmas Carol. The book was the product of a universal human impulse. It was written by a famous judge for the use of his son in the study of the law. It had and still holds the quality of fatherly advice. Poor Cowell's Dictionary, which compassed his ruin, has the distinction of having occupied the attention of King James I., both Houses of Parliament, several impressive committees, and the Court of King's Bench for upwards of a month. It was "suppressed" by proclamation under the King's hand, survived the ordeal, and in a new edition became a participant in the trial and condemnation of Archbishop Laud. Each time that it was attacked, new champions rose up in its defense. Coke's Reports were never suppressed; but they were adjudged by the King in Council and by a special committee of judges to be filled with error put there with calculated purpose. Coke was commanded to revise and correct them. This he never did, and so, if Coke really invented some of the opinions, he was not only an interpreter of law on the bench and a reporter of decisions, but in his own private person a lawgiver. Coke's Institutes also went through vicissitudes. The first, Coke Upon Littleton, was published in Coke's lifetime, but the manuscript of it, together with that of the second, third and fourth parts, was seized by Royal command while their author was on his deathbed. They were not published until ten years later, but one of them is said to have played a part in the preliminaries to the overthrow of Charles I. To Viner's Abridgment, a ponderous work produced by great industry, but yet only a humble index, the world is indebted for the establishment of the chair at Oxford which Blackstone occupied when he wrote his Commentaries. The latter, far from being unconnected with life, raised a religious and political controversy the literature of which fills a whole volume. The book itself, extravagantly praised and cordially hated, "created by repulsion the later English school of jurisprudence." Livingston's Louisiana Code, the work of a lifetime, was destroyed by fire on the very night when it was completed. The author rewrote it, and then suffered the disappointment of having it rejected by the state for which it had been prepared. Wheaton's Elements of International Law was the cause of a controversy which suspended until the present its career as an American publication. It has thus far been republished only in England.

Such events in the life of books give personality to them. They are, in themselves, characters in history, members of society, chief citizens in the commonwealth of literature.

Law books have a human appeal because of their contents and the pictures of life which form their background; because they are elemental forms of literature; because they tell the story of men and events; and because they have themselves undergone and survived vicissitudes. For other reasons, which cannot here be dwelt upon, great books of the law should be known to every cultured person. Philosophy, religion, science, the fine arts, engineering, medicine, all have their literary heroes. So has the law; and legal literature is in the first rank in point of time and of importance in the progress of human society. In the infancy of bookmaking, law and lawyers vied with theology and the priesthood. In the study of the history of printing, law books form an essential element; and in the history of thought, they challenge attention. To such names as Aristotle, Machiavelli, Bacon, Hume, Locke, Beethoven, Michael Angelo, Cellini, Shakespeare,—to select a few at random,—there must be added those of Glanville, Bracton, Littleton, Coke, Blackstone, Kent and Story.

The preceding general allegations undoubtedly need to be supported by a bill of particulars. Some such requirement the following chapters are intended to meet. But dealing with only a few books, they will not illustrate every phase of the human appeal which has been attributed to law books. The method of presentation does not admit of extended discussion either of the contents of the selected books or of their literary qualities. It does, however, allow the books to speak for themselves as personalities which have survived the test of time, and have existed as the associates of great men and events.

CHAPTER II

Cowell's Interpreter

"The lot of the dictionary maker," said Dr. Johnson, "is to be exposed to censure without hope of praise." He might have referred to the experience of John Cowell instead of his own for support of this dictum, for Cowell came near to wrecking an otherwise unblemished career when he entered the field of the lexicographer. In fact, one writer says [1] that the condemnation of his dictionary was a contributing cause to his demise, for "some other advantages they got against him, the grief whereof (hearts sunk down are not to be buoyed up) hastened his death Anno Domini 1611; and he lieth buried in Trinity Hall chapel."

The chronological record of Cowell's life can be quickly told. He was born at Ernsborough, Devonshire, in 1554, went to Eton, and thence in 1570 to King's College, Cambridge. There he studied Civil Law and became a member of Doctors' Common in 1584. In 1586 he was a proctor of the college, and in 1594 he became Regius Professor of Civil Law. In addition to his professorship, he served as Master of Trinity Hall, beginning in 1598, and from 1603 to 1604 he was Vice-Chancellor of the University. In 1608 he became Vicar-General to Archbishop Bancroft. The Regius Professorship of Civil Law at Cambridge was founded in 1540, by Henry VIII., and Cowell was the ninth incumbent of the

[1] Fuller: Worthies, 1:420.

post. He held the office from 1594 until his resignation on May 26, 1611. He died on October 11, in the same year.

Creditable as this career is, it would not entitle him to special notice in an age when he was the contemporary of such men as Shakespeare, Lord Coke, Francis Bacon, Ben Jonson, Marlowe, Bancroft and Laud. And from all evidences available, it appears that he did not seek preferment except in the line of his profession. He was a student by training and experience and not controversial by nature. But the sphere of learning in which he was skilled, the time in which he lived, the political and religious developments of the period, and the contentious character of men of the day, all combined to draw him into a vortex which made his later days a matter of public record and disturbed a whole life of academic calm. Observe the combination of circumstances: Cowell, by his appointment to the professorship of Civil Law, a post in the gift of the sovereign, came into prominence in 1594. Elizabeth was then on the throne, and by the strength of her character and the steadiness of her hand was holding in check the budding power of the Commons. She had firmly established Protestantism as the state religion, at the same time restraining the ambition of the bishops. The power of Rome and the influence of the Civil Law were waning, while the courts of Common Law were steadily growing in influence. Then came the accession of James I., a weak monarch, as compared with Elizabeth, but prepared to give to the phrase "absolute monarch" a new meaning. He meant by it not independence of all foreign or Papal interference, but freedom from all control of law—the Divine Right of Kings. He was supported in this interpretation by his bishops, who preached it from the pulpit; and were for reward raised into royal officers, with prerogatives temporal as well as religious. Thus the power of the ecclesiastical courts was strengthened while the Commons and the Common Law courts were stirred to resistance against absolutism in church and State.

In December, 1604, Bancroft was made Archbishop of Canterbury, and in 1605 Cowell, lately Vice-Chancellor of Cambridge, and then Professor of Law, and Advocate in the Arches, published his "Institutiones Juris Anglicani ad Methodum et seriem institutionum imperialium compositæ & digestæ." It was printed by John Legate at Cambridge, and on the verso of the title page bears his bookmark as printer to Cambridge University. It is a duodecimo of 268 pages, followed by an index of nine leaves. As was natural and customary for a student of the Civil Law, it is written in Latin. It is dedicated to Henry Howard, Earl of Northampton, and Chancellor of Cambridge, a famous scholar in the Civil Law, and a favorite of James I. He was the author of "A dispensation against the poison of supposed prophecies." The book contains also a prefatory address to the students of Civil Law in Trinity Hall, Cambridge. However acceptable it was to James and to Bancroft and Howard, his favorites, this book "digested into the method of the Civil and Imperial Institutes" of Rome, was probably not pleasing to the leaders of the Commons and the courts of Common Law. It did not attract unfavorable notice, however, partly because of the language in which it was written, and partly because it was in itself for the most part unobjectionable. It is a book on the Common Law of England and not on the Civil Law of Rome. The author explains that the Civil Law of England is usually called the Common Law; and his information throughout the book is drawn from the great classics of the Common Law. Not more than half a dozen times does he refer to Justinian's Institutes or any writer of Rome. His book deals with the law of persons, domestic relations, guardian and ward, real and personal property, contracts, and actions, and from time to time he compares the law of England with the law of the Continent. Nothing could be less offensive than his statement that "the precepts of the law are these, to live honestly, to do no injury to anyone, and to render everyone their due." His remarks on the prerogatives of the King are mildly stated and supported by references to English authorities. Writing in November 3, 1607 (Preface to the Interpreter), he asks indulgence for any errors in his books, excusing himself for issuing them by the desire to draw out criticisms and corrections. These he apparently had received, for "experience hath taught me," he says, "in this my Institutes lately set forth, by publishing whereof I have gained the judicious observations of divers learned gentlemen upon them; which by keeping them private I could never have procured. By which means I hope one day to commend them to you again in a more exact purity, and so leave them to future times for such acceptance as it shall please God to give them." This promised new edition he did not live to issue. The book was, however, republished long after his death in 1630, 1651, 1664 and 1676. All of the editions were in Latin except that of 1651, which was "translated into English, according to act of Parliament, for the benefit of all," by "W. G.," Esquire, and "printed by Tho: Roycroft for Jo: Ridley, at the Castle in Fleet Street, by Ram alley, London. "W. G." has not been identified. The act of

Parliament referred to was passed on November 22, 1650, entitled "An act for turning the books of the law, and all process and proceedings in Courts of Justice, into English." [2]

Apparently, up to November, 1607, no untoward results had flowed from the publication of the Institutes, and Cowell was looking forward with pleasure to issuing a new edition. In the meantime, he had devoted himself to the preparation of another work, the consequences of which were not to be so happy. This was:—

> THE INTERPRETER: or booke containing the signification of words: wherein is set foorth the true meaning of all, or the most part of such words and terms, as are mentioned in the lawe writers, or statutes of this victorious and renowned kingdome, requiring any exposition or interpretation. A worke not onely profitable, but necessary for such as desire throughly to be instructed in the knowledge of our lawes, statutes, or other antiquities. Collected by John Cowell, Doctor, and the King's Maiesties professour of the Civill Law in the Universitie of Cambridge. At Cambridge, printed by John Legate, Anno. 1607.

It is a square octavo of 292 leaves, unpaged, and bears upon its title-page Legate's bookmark. It is printed in double columns, and in alphabetical order of words, in the form of a dictionary. The definitions of the words are in English, a fact which in itself is noteworthy, because, only two years before, Cowell had written his Institutes in Latin.

The dedication is to Bancroft, "most Reverend Father in God his especial good Lord, the Lord Archbishop of Canterburie, Primate and Metropolitan of all England,

[2] Acts and Orders of the Interregnum, 2: 455–456.

and one of his Majesties most honourable Privy Council." In it he excuses himself for his presumption by recalling the fact that Bancroft had urged him to undertake the work and that it will be of service to students. "Yet the remembrance of those your fatherly provocations," he writes, "whereby, at my comming to your Grace from the Universitie, you first put me upon these studies, at the last by a kind of necessitie inforced me to this attempt: because I could not see how well to avoide it, but by adventuring the hatefull note of unthankfulnesse. For I cannot without dissimulation, but confesse my selfe perswaded, that this poore pamphlet may prove profitable to the young students of both lawes, to whose advancement that way, I have of late addicted mine indevours."

Following this dedication is an address to the readers in which Cowell offers himself to their "censures" in order that he may be admonished of his faults. He claims no originality, but says that he has "both gathered at home, and brought from abroad some ornaments for the better embellishing of our English laws." He takes as his model the civilians of other nations who "have by their mutual industries raised this kind of work in their profession, to an unexpected excellency," and particularly the recent work of Calvinus, of Heidelberg [3] who "like a laborious bee, hath gathered from all the former the best juice of their flowers, and made up a hive full of delectable hony. And by this example," he says, "would I gladly incite the learned in our Common Laws and antiquities of England, yet to lend their advice, to the gaining of some comfortable lights and prospects

[3] Calvinus, Johannes, fl. 1595–1614. Lexicon juridicum juris Romani simul, et canonici. Francofurti, 1600.

toward the beautifying of this antient palace, that hitherto hath been accompted (howsoever substantial) yet but dark and melancholy." After again asking indulgence for mistakes and omissions, due to negligence or ignorance, he explains that he has included not only words of the law, but those of any sort the meaning of which he thought to be obscure. The reason for this appears in a florid passage in which he pays tribute to the lawyer who "professeth true philosophy, and therefore should not be ignorant (if it were possible) of either beasts, fowls, or creeping things, nor of the trees from the cedar in Lebanon, to the hyssop that springeth out of the wall."

A careful examination of the Interpreter will show that Cowell did not design it to be more than a dictionary, that he drew his definitions largely from English authors and well-known Continental writers, that authority is given for practically every statement, and that few of the compiler's own opinions are to be found in the book. Nevertheless it was pleasing to Bancroft, and presumably to James I., for, on the death of Sir Edward Stanhop, March 16, 1608, creating a vacancy in the office of Vicar-General to the Archbishop, Cowell was appointed to the post. This was an important preferment, since he thus became judge of the Ecclesiastical Court. The importance of his position, and the system which he represented, including Bancroft's dogma of the Divine Right of the Episcopate, could not fail to bring him enemies who would seek opportunities for attack. One of these was Sir Edward Coke, then Chief Justice of the Court of Common Pleas. It is related that Coke always spoke of him in derision as Dr. Cow-heel; but, wrote Fuller in 1662,[4] "a *cow-heel* (I assure you) well dressed, is good

[4] Worthies, 1:420.

meat, that a cook (when hungry) may lick his fingers after it." And further, he says, "many slighted his book, who used it; it being questionable whether it gave more information or offense. Common lawyers beheld it as a double trespass against them; first, *pedibus ambulando,* that a civilian should walk in a profession *several* to themselves; secondly, that he should pluck up the pales of the hard terms wherewith it was enclosed, and lay it open and obvious to common capacities." Whether or not these were contributing causes to the attack, the book was destined to receive attention in the highest quarters, and to become the subject of political contention.

It is reported that the book gave offence because it was written to prove the excellence of the Civil Law in comparison with the Common Law of England. It was said "that the King had let fall some expressions at his table, in derogation of the latter, and highly extolling the Civil Law before it; at the same time, declaring his approbation of a book, lately writ by Dr. Cowell on that subject. This nettled the great lawyers much; and had not some of them been raised so high, that they could not, with their Court-gags, look downwards, it had bred an open contest. However, though they did not stir in it themselves, we may suppose they, underhand, stirred up this persecution against the Civilian, for fear, that if this scheme should take place, they should have their lessons to learn over again." [5] One of the titles in the book which gave greatest offense was "Littleton" who, Cowell says, "was a lawyer of great accompt, living in the daies of Edward the fourth. . . . He wrote a

[5] Parliamentary History of England, 5:222, and Kennett: Complete History of England, 2:681.

booke of great accompt called Litleton's Tenoures." This would have been very well if Cowell had stopped there but he goes on to quote Hottoman (De verbis feudalibus, word *Fœdum*) without disapproval of the uncomplimentary opinion there expressed. The passage in question, freely translated from the Latin, is the following:—"Stephen Pasquerius, a man of excellent knowledge, and leader of the faculty of Advocates at Paris, gave me a copy of Littleton's English book, which expounds the Feudal law of England so inaccurately, absurdly and stupidly that what Polidorus Virgil in his English History states, easily appears to be true, i. e., stupidity in this book contends with malice and the desire to calumniate."

It may have been injudicious to quote this extreme statement, but Cowell did not thereby make it his own, nor evince a special desire to belittle the judges of the Common Law. Nevertheless, as said by White Kennett (Preface to the 1701 ed. of the Interpreter), "the gentlemen of that robe thought themselves and their whole Faculty affronted . . . This especially gave fire to Sir Edward Coke . . . who was more particularly concerned for the honor of Littleton, and valued himself for the chief advocate of his own profession." Coke's feeling against Cowell was further increased by a matter set on foot by Archbishop Bancroft. The latter observed that the jurisdiction of the Ecclesiastical Courts was constantly obstructed by the grant of prohibitions from Westminster Hall. In order to redress this grievance he caused Cowell, his Vicar General, to draw up remonstrances or Articuli Cleri to the King. James then ordered these Articles to be argued by the judges, and Cowell's work came, therefore, under the judgment of Coke. The cases are reported by him in his own Reports (part 12, pp. 63, 65, 76), and show a genuine conflict of ideas between Bancroft and Cowell on the one hand and Coke on the other.

All of the above was but the prelude to the real attack soon to be made on the Interpreter; for, according to Kennett, Coke represented to the King that Cowell's book "disputed too nicely upon the mysteries of this his monarchy, nay in some points very derogatory to the supream power of his crown. . . . But I believe the King was wise, and the Archbishop faithful; and so this plot miscarried. Upon this disappointment," he continues, "his adversaries (who knew how to bring in a man guilty of felony, when he was acquitted of treason) turn the tables, and resolve to make him a betrayer of the rights and liberties of the people, thinking this accusation would do more with the Parliament than the other had done with the King." Kennett was speaking at a later time (1701) and in the capacity of an advocate of a man whose book he was re-editing, and therefore the above account may be special pleading. At any rate, the book was brought up in Parliament and received the attention of the King, the Lords Spiritual, the House of Lords, and the House of Commons for more than a month. This alone is sufficient to give distinction to any book; but it will be noted in the account which follows that it served also as the medium for a piece of legislative "log rolling" which is an enlightening commentary on the times. The proceedings have often been summarized, but usually with some heat and bias. It may therefore be a contribution to the subject to recount the proceedings just as they appear in the Journals of both houses, 7 and 8 James I.[6] The subject is first mentioned in the Journal of the Commons, February 24, 1609, where a committee reports that it has read Cowell's work, and found it "a book very unadvised, and undiscreet; tending to the disreputation of the honour and power of the Common Laws." Since it was "hard to censure upon a book . . . without the contexture," Mr. Martin urged the appointment of a subcommittee to "examine certain heads, wherein rashly, dangerously, perniciously" it is written, and this was agreed to. Sir Francis Bacon spoke of the "licence of the pen" as a "disease of the time" causing "poisoned opinions, disease in spirits." Such a book was objectionable not to the House alone, but to the King and the whole body, inducing misunderstandings between the King and his people. It was proposed, therefore, "to have conjunction with the Lords, for the punishment of this man." Mr. Hopkins, either to

[6] *Proceedings in Parliament concerning Cowell's book.*

(The new year, 8 James I., begins with March 25.)

Feb. 24, 1609, 1 Commons Journal, 399–400.
Feb. 26, 1609, 1 Commons Journal, 400.
Feb. 27, 1609, 2 Lords Journal, 557.
Feb. 27, 1609, 1 Commons Journal, 400.
March 2, 1609, 2 Lords Journal, 560.
March 2, 1609, 1 Commons Journal, 404.
March 3, 1609, 2 Lords Journal, 561.
March 5, 1609, 2 Lords Journal, 561–562.
March 5, 1609, 1 Commons Journal, 405–406.
March 6, 1609, 2 Lords Journal, 562.
March 7, 1609, 1 Commons Journal, 407.
March 8, 1609, 1 Commons Journal, 407.
March 8, 1609, 2 Lords Journal, 563.
March 9, 1609, 1 Commons Journal, 408.
March 10, 1609, 1 Commons Journal, 408–409.
March 27, 1610, 1 Commons Journal, 415.
March 30, 1610, 1 Commons Journal, 416.

defend Cowell, or to show that other authors also should be punished, then "produceth many other treatises containing as much as D. Cowell." On the 26th, Mr. Holt delivered a "long declamation against the opinions of D. Cowell," declaring that his offense was "not an error, indiscretion, or presumption; but a contemptuous, seditious, prodigious opinion." The Committee was directed to consider "upon what heads to confer with the Lords," and retired to the Committee Chamber, the Solicitor-General being added to the subcommittee.

For three days committee meetings, and cloak-room conferences were held, and then on February 27, 1609, it was reported in both Houses that the Lords were willing to appoint a committee to meet with a committee of the Commons to consider Cowell's book. The Lords appointed a committee of fifty, "or thereabouts," including in its members two Archbishops, thirteen Bishops, thirteen Earls, a Viscount, twenty-one Lords, and the Lords Chancellor, Treasurer, Privy Seal, Admiral and Chamberlain. To the above were added the members already appointed as Committee "touching the matter of contribution and retribution." The Lords thus indicated that they would be willing to act with the Commons in regard to Cowell, if the latter matters were taken up at the same time. The Committee appointed by the Commons consisted of the whole Privy Council, the Attorney-General, the Solicitor-General (Bacon), the Recorder and eighteen members of the Lower House. When the Lords' message was received in the Commons, there was debate on the matter of granting supplies to the King, and on wardships and tenures. The King's need for supplies was particularized and argued.[7] The Commons delayed the grant

[7] Wilson in Kennett, 2:681.

in order to put pressure on him to disavow the validity of statements in Cowell's book. "The King," it is said, "seeming much inclined to these foreign notions, and somewhat tinged with the love of arbitrary government, it is no wonder that an English Parliament began to think of clipping his wings." [8]

The joint conference was held, after the Lords had conferred with the King as to the book, and as to supplies, tenures and wardships. At the conference, the Attorney-General set forth the offenses charged against Cowell, and the Lord Bishop of London read the passages in the book under the words King, Parliament, Prerogative and Subsidy,[9] where "the said Dr. Cowell had so unadvisedly enlarged himself (as the House of Commons apprehended), that the same was very offensive and dangerous." On March 5th the results of the conference were reported by the Recorder in the Commons, where it was urged that they should not "fall to bargain;" but Sir William Strowd wished "to send to the Lords, that we can neither give support, nor supply, except the King please to treat." On the same day the Lords asked for another conference about Cowell, and on March 7th, the Commons appointed a new committee under the chairmanship of Sir Francis Bacon to prepare for this second joint conference. On the 8th, Mr. Martin urged in the Commons that the Conference should only hear and report, and that the two Houses join in asking His Majesty's leave to proceed with Dr. Cowell. The Lords should be questioned what offense Cowell had committed, whether exemplary punishment should be meted out to him, and what course should be taken to suppress the

[8] Parliamentary History of England, 5: 222.

[9] See end of this chapter for the passages in question.

book. On the same day (8th) in the Upper House, the Lord Chancellor referred to the proposed conference, and reported that "His Majesty had taken notice of the matter, and had lately perused the places in the book whereunto exceptions were taken; and had called the said Cowell before him, and heard his answer thereunto." The Lord Treasurer then delivered to the Lords the King's decision, and was appointed to report the same to the Conference. Three Lords were also appointed to report on what was said by the subcommittee of the Commons on wards and tenures. After the Conference report was made to the Commons (March 10th). Here are some of the disjointed passages from the Journal:— "That the King had taken notice of the book—It was not neglected—They did respect offenses done severally and respectively—That the proceeding was concurrent— The King—Called the party:—examined—That this man had been too bold—That is a presumption in any subject—as we are curious—No wrong to the King—A tender thing to submit the King to certain definition . . . The King will suppress the book; did hate him that defended it . . . Happy we have a man to our King . . . That the Lords would join with us in punishment of the offender." The next mention of Cowell in the Journals is on March 27th, when the King's proclamation respecting the book was read in the Commons. The Chancellor was directed to "go and give thanks presently to his Majesty," which he did, and on his return he reported that he had acquainted the King of "the joyful acceptation of the proclamation," and had promised that he would ever maintain the Common Laws of the land.

"Answ. by His Majesty:—Very glad, the eucharistique

days were not yet ended—As great comfort in thanks, as you in love and favour. That whatsoever he spoke to themselves, or to Mr. Speaker, he will ever stand to in publick which he spoke in private."

The last reference in the Journals is on March 30, when Sir George Moore reported the registering of the proclamation. This proclamation is not given in the Journals of Parliament, but what purports to be a copy of it is printed in the preface to Kennett's edition of the Interpreter, 1701, as follows:—

A PROCLAMATION touching Dr. Cowell's Book called the Interpreter.

"This later Age and Times of the World wherein we are fallen, is so much given to verbal profession, as well of Religion, as of all commendable Royal Virtues, but wanting the Actions and Deeds agreeable to so specious a profession, as it hath bred such an unsatiable curiosity in many men's spirits, and such an itching in the tongues and pens of most men, as nothing is left unsearched to the bottom both in talking and writing. For from the very highest mysterys in the Godhead and the most inscrutable counsels in the Trinity, to the very lowest pit of hell, and the confused actions of the devils there; there is nothing now unsearched into by the curiosity of men's brains. Men not being contented with the knowledge of so much of the will of God as it hath pleased Him to reveal; but they will need sit with Him in His most private closet and become privy of His most inscrutable counsels; and therefore, it is no wonder, that men in these our days do not spare to wade in all the deepest mysteries that belong to the persons or state of kings and princes, that are Gods upon earth; since we see (as we have already said) that they spare not God Himself. And this license that every talker or writer now assumeth to himself, is come to this abuse, that many Phormios will give counsel to Hannibal, and many men that never went out of the compass of cloysters or colleges will freely wade by their writings in the deepest mysteries of monarchy and political government: whereupon, it cannot otherwise fall out, but that when men go out of their element, and meddle with things above their capacity; themselves shall not only go astray and stumble in darkness, but will mislead also divers others with themselves into many mistakings and errors; the proof whereof we have lately had by a book written by Dr. Cowell called the Interpreter: for he being only a civilian by profession, and upon that large ground of a kind of dictionary (as it were) following the alphabet, having all kind of purposes belonging to government and monarchy in his way, by meddling in matters above his reach, he hath fallen in many things to mistake and deceive himself: in some things disputing so nicely upon the mysteries of this our monarchy, that it may receive doubtful interpretations: yea in some points very derogatory to the supreme power of this Crown: in other cases mistaking the true state of the Parliament of this Kingdom, and the fundamental constitutions and privileges thereof: and in some other points speaking unreverently of the Common Law of England, and the works of some of the most famous and ancient judges therein: it being a thing utterly unlawful to any subject, to speak or write against that law under which he liveth, and which we are sworn and are resolved to maintain. Wherefore upon just considerations moving us hereunto, for preventing of the said errors and inconveniences in all times to come, we do hereby not only prohibit the buying, uttering, or reading of the said book, but do also will and straitly command all and singular persons whatsoever, who have or shall have any of them in their hands or custody, that upon pain of our high displeasure, and the consequence thereof, they do deliver the same presently upon this publication to the Lord Mayor of London, if they or any of them be dwelling in or near the said city, or otherwise to the sheriff of the county where they or any of them shall reside, and in the two universities to the Chancellor or Vice-Chancellor there, to the intent that further order may be given for the utter suppressing thereof. And because there shall be better oversight of books of all sorts before they come to the press, we have resolved to make choice of Commissioners, that shall look more narrowly into the nature of all those things that shall be put to the press, either concerning our authority Royal, or concerning our government, or the laws of our Kingdom, from whom a more strict account shall be yielded unto us, than hath been used heretofore.

"Given at our Palace of Westminster the 25th day of March, in the Eighth year of our reign, of Great Brittain, France and Ireland. Anno. Dom. 1610."

It has repeatedly been stated that the book, after all copies had been called in, was burnt by the common hangman. I find no verification of this, and certainly it was not ordered by the above proclamation. Moreover, many copies of this first edition are still extant in the law libraries of England and the United States. It was not much easier to suppress a published book in 1610 than it is to-day, a fact which is referred to in connection with this book by Roger Coke.[10] He says that Cowell wrote the book to supply the King's necessities, "no doubt set upon by Bancroft and those called the Church." "The Commons," he continues, "though they took no notice of Bancroft and his Articles against Prohibitions, took fire at these [Cowell's statements], and intended to have proceeded severely against him, but the King interposed, and promised to call in these books by proclamation, as he did, but they were out, and the proclamation could not call them in, but only served to make them more taken notice of: But this had not the desired effect of getting more money, than one subsidy, and one-tenth, whereupon the King, by proclamation dissolved them the 31st December, 1609 (*sic.*), after they had sat near seven years."

Kennett (Preface, 1701) admits that the books could not be called in, but says that this statement is "the only truth that drops from that gentleman [Roger Coke] in his relation of this matter." And after some evidences of inaccuracy or lack of truth, he continues, "Roger Coke, Esq., was descended from the Lord Chief Justice, and so by right of inheritance had a fewd against Dr. Cowell, and by the same hereditary right was to be no good historian; for that Oracle of the Law, was at least no Oracle in matters of fact. His opinions may be excellent, but his stories are most of them trifles and falsehood."

We have now brought the story of Cowell and his Interpreter down to March 30, 1610. No exemplary punishment was visited upon him, and he had been put under physical restraint only to the extent of being committed to an Alderman's house during the progress of the in-

[10] Detection, 1696, Book 1, pp. 30–31.

vestigation.[11] But he had been made a scapegoat by the King, and was soon to lose the protection of Bancroft who died on November 2, 1610. Therefore, according to Kennett, "like a wise man he took his leave of the press, and retired to his colledge, and his private studies." Thus the world was deprived of a book which he had promised in the preface to his Interpreter, where he says: "I have in some towardness a tract (De Regulis Juris) wherein my intent is, by collating the cases of both lawes, to shewe, that they both be raised of one foundation, and differ more in language and termes then in substance, and therefore were they reduced to one methode (as they easily might) to be attained (in a maner) with all one paines. But my time imparted to these studies, being stolne from mine emploiments of greater necessitie, I cannot make the hast I desire, or perhaps that the discourse may deserve. Wherefore until my leisure may serve to performe that, I intreate you lovingly to accept this." He resigned his professorship on May 26, 1611, and died "upon the operation of being cut for the stone," on October 11.

With the great array of forces against it, it might now be supposed that The Interpreter was dead along with its author. But as Roger Coke said, the book was out and could not be recalled by proclamation. That a man's works live after him is truly shown by Cowell's dictionary. Not only did many copies remain in the hands of readers, not only was it reprinted when the supply was exhausted after the lapse of thirty years, but this reprinting was an offense charged against a character as famous in English history as James I., Coke, or Ban-

[11] Winwood: Memorials, 3: 137.

croft. This was William Laud, Archbishop of Canterbury from 1633, and beheaded for treason in 1645.

In 1637, the Interpreter was reprinted verbatim and with almost identical size, type and form, under the imprint of William Sheares, London. The latter was one of the most reputable booksellers of the time, having shops in various parts of London, and being publisher of much of the best literature of the period. He was, however, suspected of having had a hand in printing Leicester's Commonwealth, a notorious satire on the House of Lords. As will presently be seen he was the publisher, though not the printer, of the 1637 edition of the Interpreter. The contest between the King and the Commons having been carried over into the reign of Charles I., Laud, early accused of desiring to introduce the doctrines of Rome into the Church, stood with Charles against the Lower House, taking occasion in sermons preached before his first and second Parliaments to magnify the King's authority in the State as well as in the Church. While Charles was governing without a Parliament, from 1629 to 1640, Laud came to great power and influence in the State both as spiritual and temporal adviser to the King. In 1638 Civil War broke out in Scotland over the ecclesiastical policy of Charles and Laud, as a result of which Charles was forced to summon the Long Parliament. One of its first acts was to impeach Laud for treason (December 18, 1640). He was committed to the Tower March 1, 1641, but his trial did not begin until March 12, 1644. It was then that he was charged with having connived at the reprinting of Cowell's book in 1637. Licenses to print books were then in the gift of Laud, and so a case could be made out against him of neglect of duty. Whether he secretly permitted the reissuing of the book or not, it is certain that he signed an order on October 8, 1638, recalling the edition.[12] At any rate, Cowell's book figures prominently in the charges against Laud. The matter came up on the opening day of the trial, March 12, 1644/3, when Sergeant Wilde accused him of having caused sermons to be preached in Court to set the King's prerogative above the law, "and books to be printed to the same effect." The Journals of the House of Commons [13] set forth the proceedings of the next day as follows:—

"And first was produced a book called "Cowell's Interpreter, which, in the title King, hath the words to this effect, 'That the King is above the law, by His *absolute,* etc.' And in the title of Prerogative, 'That He hath a prerogative above the law, etc.;' which said book, by judgment of Parliament, was condemned, and called in by a proclamation, dated 1610, in Parliament, and an inhibition that none should be sold or published; yet, notwithstanding this, in scorn and contempt of the Parliament, the said book was reprinted in *Duck Lane,* at a private house, by one Hodskins, printer to the Archbishop, without any order of license; and, upon complaint thereof to the Archbishop, by Joseph Hunscott and [ ] Wally, he put them off to Sir John Lambe, and he to the printer; who said, 'The Proclamation was made in a schismatical and scandalous Parliament time.' And the Archbishop told the said Hunscott when he came to him about it, 'That, if he would not go his way, he would trounce him.'" Laud's answer to these charges may best be

[12] Tanner's Mss. 67:25, cited in Troubles and Trial of Laud, 4: 78n.

[13] 6:468, 19 Ch. I, March 13, 1644/3.

given in his own words:[14] "Then was charged upon me," he writes, "the printing of books, which asserted the King's Prerogative above law, etc. The instance was in Dr. Cowell's Book, *Verbo Rex*. That this book was decried by proclamation; that complaint was made to me, that this book was printing in a close house without license, and by Hodgkinson,[15] who was my printer; that I referred them to Sir. John Lambe; that they came to me again, and a third time, and I still continued my reference; which Sir John Lambe slighting, the book came forth. The witnesses to this were Hunt and Walye, if I mistook not their names.

"1. For this book of Dr. Cowell's, I never knew of it till it was printed, or so far gone on in printing, that I could not stay it; and the witnesses say 'it was in a close house and without license,' so neither I nor my chaplains could take notice of it.

"2. They say, they informed me of it, but name no time, but only the year 1638. But they confess I was then at Croydon; so being out of town (as were almost all the High Commissioners) I required Sir John Lambe who being a High Commissioner, had in that business as much power as myself, to look to it carefully, that the book proceeded not; or if it were already printed, that it came not forth. If Sir John slighted his own duty and my command (as themselves say) he is living and may

[14] Troubles and Trial of Laud, 4:78–80, Library of Anglo-Catholic Theology.

[15] Richard Hodgkinson, printer, was in 1635 investigated by the Star Chamber, and his press and type seized, but on recommendation of the Commissioners, they were returned to him. His connection with the printing of Cowell's Interpreter did not prevent him from being chosen one of the twenty printers appointed under Act of Parliament.

answer for himself; and I hope your Lordships will not put his neglect on my account.

"3. As for Hodgkinson he was never my printer, but Badger was the man I employed, as is well known to all the Stationers; nor was Hodgkinson ever employed by me in that kind or any other; upon just complaint, I turned him out of a place, but never put him into any: and therefore, those terms which were put upon me of 'my Hodgkinson' and 'my Sir John Lambe,' might have been spared. Sir John was indeed Dean of the Arches, and I imployed him as other Archbishops did the Deans which were in their times; otherwise no way mine: and Hodgkinson had his whole dependence on Sir Henry Martin, and was a mere stranger to me. And this answer I gave to Mr. Browne, when he summed up the charge. Nor could any danger be in the printing of that book to mislead any man: because it was generally made known by proclamation, that it was a book condemned, and in such particulars: but for other things the book was very useful."

Although the Interpreter cannot be said to have had a deciding voice in the condemnation of Laud, it was itself by these proceedings a second time officially condemned. Nevertheless, it arose like a Phœnix from its own ashes, and was republished unchanged in 1658. It bears the imprint of a reputable printer, Francis Leach, and the names of three well-known law-book sellers, Henry Twyford, Thomas Dring and John Place. Who was responsible for this edition I do not know, since there is no new preface, Cowell's dedication and preface being reprinted *verbatim*. The quotation from Hottoman about Littleton is retained, as well as the statements under the words King, Parliament, Prerogative and Subsidy to which so much objection had been made. Evidently Cromwell, then in the height of his power, was in no degree averse to definitions which exalted the position of the actual head of the State.

Thus far no one had had the courage to associate his name with Cowell's in the capacity of editor. In 1672, however, Thomas Manley, of the Middle Temple, became sponsor for a new edition. He was the author of several law books, and is said to have given "considerable aid to the movement, which received its impetus from James I., for the use of English instead of Latin in legal literature." He issued a second edition in 1684. Manley's first edition appeared in the same year that Charles II. ordered that all manner of penal laws on matters ecclesiastical against whatever sort of nonconformists or recusants should be suspended. There was a general movement toward freedom of the press, which culminated in the expiration in 1679 of the statute, passed immediately after the Restoration, regulating printing. Perhaps these facts account for the new edition of the book and for the defence of Cowell contained in the preface. The groundwork upon which I build," says Manley, "is Cowell's Interpreter, an excellent book both as to its matter and composure, and did not deserve that severe arraignment that it hath of late suffered: those intermixtures of his in the Civil Law being absolutely necessary to be known by him who would have the repute of a learned and well-read Common Lawyer; and his few defects (for they are not many for so great an undertaking) might, at least, after so many years have been passed over in silence. And let others boast of themselves what they please; I am not ashamed to own him, and to acknowledge, that I only follow and make more publickly useful that path which his industry first laid open to us: Wherein to use his own words, "That whoever shall observe most faults therein, I, by gleaning after, will collect as many omitted by him, as he shall shew committed by me." (Preface to editions of 1672 and 1684.) The first of Manley's editions, the preface of which is dated October 23, 1671, was dedicated to Anthony Lord Ashley, Baron of Wimborne St. Giles, Chancellor of the Exchequer, and member of the Privy Council. This fact, together with the impressive array of publishers whose names appear in the imprint, makes it certain that the book was now considered unexceptionable. Manley contributed to this result by omitting several matters which he said were "unfit for the time," and he did in fact omit the expressions under the words Parliament, Prerogative and Subsidy, to which objection had been raised. Under the word King, however, he substituted phrases which would have been the undoing of Cowell.[16] The quotation from Hottoman does not appear in this edition. Both of Manley's editions are in folio, double columns, and are amplified with an "Appendix containing the ancient names of places here in England, very necessary for the use of all young students, who intend to converse with old records, deeds or charters." [17]

When a book arrives at the estate of mere respectability, it will not long survive unless it has genuine worth. Cowell's Interpreter was now respectable and of venerable age. It had weathered the storms of three

[16] See quotations at the end of this chapter.

[17] A copy of the 1684 edition in the Columbia University Law Library bears on the title page the autograph of John Jay, Chief Justice of the United States.

quarters of a century. It had seen kings and parliaments and protectors, with their prerogatives and subsidies come and go; and it had played its part sturdily in great political events of a stirring period. It was still both profitable and necessary to lawyers and to all who would "not be ignorant . . . of either beasts, fowls, or creeping things, nor of the trees from the cedar in Lebanon, to the hyssop that springeth out of the wall." It needed no further defense, but nevertheless was destined to receive it at the hands of one of the prominent ecclesiastical figures of the first quarter of the eighteenth century. This was White Kennett, whom Pope had in mind when he wrote the lines:—

> "Then unbelieving priests reformed the nation,
> And taught more pleasing methods of salvation."

Kennett was famous as a controversial writer on the affairs of the Church, and, though the subject of bitter attack, he rose to be Bishop of Peterborough. His reputation to-day rests chiefly on his antiquarian researches which are embodied in many printed books and manuscripts.[18] He was, according to Philip Bliss, editor of Wood's Fasti Oxonienses (London, 1815, Pt. 1, Column 289) the editor of the 1701 edition of Cowell's Interpreter. The fact is not mentioned by Kennett's biographer, William Newton,[19] and his name nowhere appears in the Interpreter itself. Whether the latter omission was to avoid further strife in an already troubled career I do not know, but undoubtedly his interest in the work

[18] Complete History of England; Parochial Antiquities; Register and Chronicle, Ecclesiastical and Civil; Bibliothecæ Americanæ primordia.

[19] Life of the Right Reverend Dr. White Kennett. London, 1730.

was twofold. He was already the author of a "Glossary to Explain the Original, the Acceptation and Obsoleteness of Words and Phrases" (London, 1695), and from his independent researches was well equipped to augment Cowell's work by adding "many thousand words . . . as are found in our histories, antiquities, cartularies, rolls, registers, and other manuscript records, not hitherto explained in any dictionary." On the other hand, he was in 1701 a pronounced Royalist, and probably welcomed the opportunity of giving new life to a work which had been the victim of the House of Commons. He made himself the champion for Cowell and his book, writing an extensive preface in which their detractors are pictured in no favorable light. It is the work of a propagandist as well as of an editor.

Two other editions of the Interpreter were printed, both in the lifetime of Kennett, who died in 1728. The edition of 1708 differs in no way from that of 1701, except in a transposition of words in the title; but the 1727 edition is considerably enlarged. Both of these editions retain Kennett's preface, with an added paragraph in the latter. These two editions have not previously been accredited to Kennett, but appear to the writer to be the work of his hand.

Thus ends the story of Cowell's Interpreter, but not of its influence in the world of English law books. It was the third law dictionary in order of time issuing out of the British Isles. It was preceded by "Expositiones Terminorum Legum Anglorum," published in two editions, one in Latin and one in English, in 1527; and by Skene's "De Verborum Significatione, or Exposition of the Difficil Termes in the foure Books of Regiam Majestatem," a glossary of Scotch law, published in Edinburgh in 1597. All other English law dictionaries are based on these three works. A dictionary, said Kennett (Preface to the Interpreter), "is no more to be raised up in one impression, than Rome in a day. What have all sorts of glossaries and dictionaries been at the first projecting of them but rude and modelling draughts, but meer scaffolding to carry up materials, to build higher and higher in due time and order." Substantial scaffolding these three books were for the erection of the modern law dictionary; and Cowell's humble work would have been worthy of study even though it had not had such an eventful history.

Excerpts from Cowell's Interpreter

(Passages in brackets [ ] were omitted in Manley's edition, 1672.)

KING (REX) is thought by M. Camden, in his Britan. pag. 105, to be contracted of the Saxon word Cyninge, signifiing him that hath the highest power & absolute rule ouer our whole Land, and thereupon the King is in intendment of Lawe cleared of those defects, that common persons be subject vnto. For he is alwaies supposed to be of full age, though he be in yeares neuer so young. Cromptons Jurisdictions. fol. 134. Kitchin. fol. 1. He is taken as not subject to death, but is a Corporation in himselfe that liueth euer. Crompton ibidem. Thirdly, he is aboue the Law by his absolute power. Bracton lib. pri cap. 8. Kitchin fol. 1. And though for the beter and equall course in making Lawes he doe admitte the 3 estates, that is Lords Spirituall, Lords temporall, and the Commons vnto Councell: yet this, [in diuers lerned mens opinions, is not of constreinte, but of his owne benignitie, or by reason of his promise made vpon oath, at the time of his coronation. For otherwise were he a subject after a sort and subordinate, which may not bee thought without breach of duty and loyaltie. For then must we deny him to be aboue the lawe, and to haue no power of dispensing with any positiue lawe, or of graunting especiall priuiledges and charters vnto any, which is his onely and cleare right, as Sir Thomas Smith well expresseth lib. 2. cap. 3. de Repub. Anglican. and Bracton, lib. 2. cap. 16, num. 3. and Britton, cap. 39.] (Manley substitutes the following: "Yet this derogates not from his power; for whatever they act, he by his negative voyce may quash") For hee pardoneth life and limme to offendours against his crowne and dignitie, except such as he bindeth himself by oath not to forgiue. Stawnf. pl. cor. lib. 2. cap. 35. And Habet omnia iura in manu sua. Bracton, lib. 2. cap. 24. num. prim. [And though at his coronation he take an oath not to alter the lawes of the land: Yet this oath notwithstanding,] hee may alter or suspend any particular lawe that seemeth hurtfull to the publike estate. Blackwood in Apologia Regum, c. 11. See Oath of the King. [Thus much in short, because I haue heard some to be of opinion, that the lawes be aboue the king. But the kings oath of old you may see in Bracton, lib. 3. cap. 9. nu. 2. for the which looke in Oath of the King. The kings oath in English, you may see in the old abridgement of Statutes, titulo, Sacram. Regis. Fourthly,] the kings only testimonie of any thing done in his presence, is of as high nature and credit as any Record. Whence it cometh, that in all writs or precepts sent out for the dispatch of Iustice, he vseth none other witnesse but himselfe, alwaies vsing these words vnder it, Teste me ipso. Lastly, he hath in the right of his crowne many prerogatiues aboue any common person, be he neuer so potent or honourable: whereof you may reade your fill in Stawnf. tractate vpon the Statute thereof made, anno. 17. Ed. 2. though that containe not all by a great number. What the kings power is, reade in Bracton, lib. 2. cap. 24. nu. prim. & 2.

PARLIAMENT . . . [Touching the great authoritie of this court, I find in Stowes Annals pag. 660, that Henry the sixth directing his priuie seale to Richard Earle of Warwicke, thereby to discharge him of the Captainship of Cales, the Earle refused to obey the priuie seale, and continued forth the said office, because he receiued it by Parlament. But one example cannot make good a doctrine. And of these two one must needes be true, that either the king is aboue the Parlament, that is, the positiue lawes of his kingdome, or els that he is not an absolute king. Aristotle lib. 3. Politico. cap. 16. And therefore though it be a mercifull policie, and also a politique mercie (not alterable without great perill) to make lawes by the consent of the whole Realme, because so no one part shall haue cause to complaine of a partialitie: yet simply to binde the prince to or by these lawes weare repugnant to the nature and constitution of an absolute monarchy.] Omitted by Manley.

PREROGATIUE of the king (prerogatiua regis) is that especiall power, preeminence, or priuiledge that the King hath in any kinde, ouer and aboue other persons, and aboue the ordinarie course of the common lawe, in the right of his crowne. And this word (Prerogatiua) is vsed by the Ciuilians in the same sense 1. Rescriptum. 6. § 4. de bono. & muner. . . . [Now for those regalities which are of the higher nature (all being within the compas of his prerogatiue, and iustly to be comprised vnder that title) there is not one that belonged to the most absolute prince in the world, which doth not also belong to our king, except the customes of the nations so differ (as indeede they doe) that one thing be in the one accompted a regalitie, that in another is none. Onely by the custome of this kingdome, he maketh no lawes without the consent of the 3 estates though he may quash any lawe concluded of by them. And whether his power of making lawes be restreined (de necessitate) or of a godly and commendable policy, not to be altered without great perill, I leaue to the iudgment of wiser men. But I hold it incontrowlable, that the king of England is an absolute king.]

SUBSIDIE, (subsidium) commeth of the French (subside) signifying a taxe or tribute assessed by Parlament, and graunted by the commons to be leuied of euery subject, [according to the value of his lands or goods after the rate of 4. shillings in the pound for land, and 2. shillings 8. pence for goods, as it is most commonly vsed at this day. Some hold opinion, that this subsidie is graunted by the subject to the Prince, in recompence or consideration, that whereas the Prince of his absolute power, might make lawes of himselfe, he doth of fauour admit the consent of his subjects therein, that all things in their owne confession may be done with the greater indifferencie.]

Sir Edward Coke

CHAPTER III

Lord Coke and The Reports

"There is no jewel in the world comparable to learning; no learning so excellent both for prince and subject as knowledge of laws; and no knowledge of any laws (I speak of human) so necessary for all estates and for all causes, concerning goods, lands, or life as the Common Laws of England." [1] Here, in one sentence, we have the motive for all of Sir Edward Coke's legal writings, and for the whole of his judicial career. It is a sentiment which might have come from a recluse whose enthusiasm, drawn from researches in musty folios, had not been dampened by contact with the world. It came, however, from a man who for nearly fifty years held public office, and either as lawyer, judge or politician, participated in the great events of his time. He was so great a figure that the records of his period are filled with references to him and to the controversies which centered about him. The span of his life covered the whole of the reigns of three sovereigns, Mary, Elizabeth, and James I., and part of the reign of Charles I. During his whole manhood he was a public personage.[2]

[1] Coke's Reports, Part 2, preface.

[2] Born February 1, 1552; entered Trinity College, Cambridge, 1567; student at the Inner Temple, 1572; called to the Bar, 1578; Reader in Lyon's Inn, 1578-80; Recorder of Coventry, 1585; Recorder of Norwich, 1586; Bencher of Inner Temple, 1590; Recorder of London, 1592; Solicitor-General, 1592; Reader to Inner Temple, 1592; Member from Norfolk, 1592; Speaker House of Commons, 1592-93; Attorney-General, 1593; Knighted, 1603; Chief Justice of

And yet he wrote two great legal works which might well have been the product of a lifetime largely devoted to scholarship. He excelled not only in rendering but in recording judicial decisions, and he has also to his credit the first comprehensive work on the laws of England. So much is there to be said about his Reports, on the one hand, and his Institutes on the other, that they must here be treated in separate chapters. (See Chapter IV.)

The story of Coke's Reports runs from the year 1580 to the present day, for they are still living books of the law. The eleven parts published during his lifetime furnished the chief literary labor for nearly the whole of his career as a lawyer. After being called to the Bar, his rise to a lucrative practice was rapid, not only on account of intense application to study, but because of the position and wealth of his family. His father, Robert Coke, had been a bencher of Lincoln's Inn, and a well-known barrister. His mother, Winifred Knightley, had inherited considerable property; and Coke himself early began the acquisition of property by purchase—a practice which later, it is said, led James I. to tell him, when he was about to purchase Castle Acre Priory, that he already had as much land as it was proper for a subject to possess. Coke replied, "Then, please your Majesty, I will only add one *acre* more to my estate." The first part of his Reports was not published until 1600, but we know from the preface that he began preparing them in the twenty-

Court of Common Pleas, 1606; Chief Justice Court of King's Bench, 1613; Member of Privy Council, 1613; High Steward of Cambridge University, 1614; suspended from Chief-Justiceship, 1616; removed from office, Nov. 15, 1616; recalled to King's Council, 1617; Member from Liskeard, 1620; imprisoned in Tower, 1622; Member from Coventry, 1624; Member from Norfolk, 1626; Member from Buckingham, 1628; died, September 3, 1634.

second year of Elizabeth's reign. At this time the only law reports that had been published were the Year Books, Plowden's Commentaries, 1571, and Dyer's Reports, 1585. Leaving out of consideration the Year Books, Coke's Reports were third in order of time, and during his life no others appeared. Plowden had started the practice followed by many later reporters of asserting in their prefaces that when compiling their Reports, they had no intention of publishing them. So common did this practice become of assuming the pose of excessive modesty and reluctance to becoming an author that its expression was reduced almost to a form. Plowden first tells what led him to begin noting down cases which he heard in court, and then continues, "This work I originally entered upon with a view to my own private instruction only, without the least thought or intention of letting it appear in print." He was, however, urged by some "grave and learned men" of the law to publish the reports, and was diffidently and doubtfully considering the proposition when "by and by an accident happened, which inclined me," he says, "and (as I may say) forcibly compelled me to make this work public." This "accident" was the lending of the manuscript to his intimate friends, whose clerks "made such expedition, by writing day and night, that in a short time they had transcribed a great number of the cases . . . contrary to my knowledge and intent, or of those to whom I had lent the book." These copies, which were defective, incomplete and incorrect, came into the hands of printers who intended to publish them for profit. Therefore, in self-defense, Plowden began to reconsider his decision not to publish them himself, and at the same time was urged to do so by all the judges of both benches, and by the Barons of the Exchequer. "And at last," he says, "upon these and other motives, and hoping that it might be of some benefit to the students of the law, I resolved (as you see I have done) to put it in print." Dyer did not himself publish his Reports, but when he died in 1582, left them by will to his nephew, Richard Farwell, who with another nephew, James Dyer, issued them in 1585. The nephews protest that they had no intention or desire to publish the Reports. But when they were shown to "some of our loving friends . . . the opinion they had of the author of this work, together with the excellency thereof . . . seemed to enflame them with desire to have the same, as that the books themselves or the copies thereof without breach of friendship might not be denied them." Then, being importuned to have the books printed, they resisted for two years, but finally yielded.

Coke gives us a somewhat different reason for printing, less modest, but resting on the high ground of service to the Queen and to coming generations of lawyers and judges. "I have since the 22d year of her Majesty's reign," he says, "which is now twenty years complete, observed the true reasons, as near as I could, of such matters in law (wherein I was of counsel, and acquainted with the state of the question) as have been adjudged upon great and mature deliberation; and as I never meant (as many have found) to keep them so secret for my own private use, as to deny the request of any friend to have either view or copy of any of them: so till of late I never could be persuaded (as many can witness) to make them so public, as by any entreaty to commit them to print: but when I considered how by her Majesty's princely care and choice, her seats of justice have been ever for the due execution of her laws, furnished with judges of such excellent knowledge and wisdom (whereunto they have attained in this fruitful springtime of her blessed reign) as I fear that succeeding ages shall not afford successors equal unto them, I have adventured to publish certain of their resolutions (in such sort as my little leisure would permit) for the help of their memory who heard them, and perfectly knew them, for the instruction of others who knew them not, but imperfectly heard of them; and lastly, for the common good (for that is my chief purpose), in quieting and establishing of the possessions of many in these general cases, wherein there hath been such variety of opinions." "Memorable things," he says, "should be committed to writing . . . and not wholly be taken to slippery memory, which seldom yieldeth a certain reckoning." This dictum he supports by examples of injustice done because precedents were not available or were neglected.

Coke seems to think it his duty to explain why he continued to issue his successive "editions," as he calls the parts of his Reports. Again and again he says in his prefaces that he intends them only to serve the common good, and to quiet enjoyment of rights and property by the resolution of doubts raised by diversity of opinions among the judges. He is not unmindful of the praise which his efforts have received. In his third preface, for instance, he says: "Your extraordinary allowance of my last Reports, being freshly accompanied with new desires, have overcome me to publish these few excellent judgments and resolutions of the reverend judges and sages of the law." The "new desires" came not from lawyers alone, but from the King himself whose commands required Coke to proceed and, he says, "imposed a necessity upon me to publish this fourth edition." This official sanction is mentioned again in the seventh preface, where he disclaims any intention of publishing his private notes of one of the cases, but then found that (he says) "I was by commandment to begin again for the public." The title pages themselves invariably speak in laudatory terms of either Elizabeth or James I., and the preface to the eleventh part, published while Coke was under a cloud, ends with the protestation that "the end of this edition is, that God may be glorified, his Majesty honoured, the common good encreased; the learned confirmed, and the student instructed." These reasons for publication, asserted over a period of fifteen years, are significant when put side by side with the accusation subsequently made against these same Reports.

The Reports provide a record of one side of Coke's career as a lawyer and judge. The first five parts were published while he was Attorney-General (1593–1606), first to Queen Elizabeth, and second to King James I.; the sixth to the ninth parts, while he was Lord Chief Justice of the Common Pleas (1606–1613); and the tenth and eleventh parts while he was Lord Chief Justice of the King's Bench (1613–1616). Many of the cases reported were those in which he had a prominent part either as counsel, prosecutor or judge. The prefaces, hereafter to be described, are made up mostly of matter interesting only to the lawyer, but they throw light also on the environment in which lawyers worked, the way in which they were trained, their attitude toward laymen, particularly "historians" and "chroniclers," and they are themselves examples of a style of writing which was common in Coke's day.

The record of another side of Coke's legal career is found in the letters of his chief rival, Sir Francis Bacon. The careers of these two men run nearly parallel, and the story of the Reports is one of the transverse connections between them. Coke was born in 1552 and Bacon in 1561. Both men almost continuously held public office, both rose to the height of their ambition and both suffered downfall a few years thereafter. Bacon fell, however, never to rise, while Coke soon was "on foot" again, and in a position of authority and power. Coke was first in the field and last to leave it. He became Solicitor-General in 1592; Bacon in 1607. Coke was Attorney-General from 1593 to 1606; Bacon from 1613 to 1617. Coke was Chief-Justice of the Common Pleas from 1606 to 1613 and Chief Justice of the King's Bench from 1613 to 1616, when he was removed from office largely through Bacon's influence. Bacon was made Baron Verulam in 1618 and Viscount St. Albans in 1620. He attained to the headship of the Court of Chancery with title of Lord Keeper of the Privy Seal in 1617, an office which he held until 1621 when he was impeached for corruption. In the meantime, Coke had regained the royal favor and been recalled to the King's Council, and at Bacon's downfall he was a member of Parliament.[3] During all of this period these two men were constantly thrown together, took part in the same public events,

[3] The parallel appears clearly in the following chronology:

Coke.		*Bacon*	
1552.	Born.	1561.	Born.
1592.	Solicitor-General.		
1593.	Attorney-General.		
1598.	Married Lady Hatton.	1598.	Unsuccessful suitor for Lady Hatton's hand.
1606.	Chief Justice of Common Pleas.	1607.	Solicitor-General.

(Continued on next page)

gained advantages over each other, and consistently represented two opposing sides in a long controversy important in the history of English legal institutions.

The eleventh part of Coke's Reports, according to the title page, was published in the year 1615, "the thirteenth year of the most high and most illustrious James, King of England, France and Ireland, and of Scotland the XLIX., the Fountain of all Piety and Justice, and the Life of the Law." "This eleventh work," says Coke in his preface, "I have published in the tempest of many other important and pressing business; and therefore could not polish them as I desired." The pressing business referred to may have been extraordinary duties as Privy Councilor and judge, but it is more than probable that he had in mind questions which had arisen bearing on the jurisdiction and powers of the court over which he presided,—questions which to him were of primary importance, not merely because they appeared to have been raised at the instigation of Bacon, but because they were likely to affect the whole course of judicial development in England. Spedding is undoubtedly correct when he says of Coke[4] that his ruling passion always was "the assertion and enforcement of the

Coke.		*Bacon.*	
1613.	Chief Justice King's Bench. Privy Councilor.	1613.	Attorney-General.
1616.	Removed.	1616.	Privy Councilor.
1617.	Recalled to Privy Council.	1617.	Lord Keeper.
		1618.	Created Baron Verulam and Lord Chancellor.
1620.	In Parliament.	1620.	Viscount St. Albans.
		1621.	Tried for bribery and removed from office.
1634.	Died.	1626.	Died.

[4] Letters and life of Bacon, 7: 194.

authority of his own office for the time being,"—an attitude likely to make for him many enemies, and subject to criticism anything that he might say or do. But there is no reason to suspect that he was insincere in fighting for the prerogatives of his court. He believed it to have precedence over all other courts, including the Court of Chancery. When, on the title pages of the two last parts of his Reports, he described himself as "Lord Chief Justice of England," he used the same expression by which he had characterized Sir Christopher Wray, when the latter was Chief Justice of the King's Bench. In this instance, history must acquit him of the charge of self-aggrandizement; but his enthusiasm and combative temperament made him willing to go to great lengths in maintaining his position. Thereby, he gave opportunity to his rivals.

Two well-known episodes led up to his removal from office. One was the case of Commendams.[5] One of the ancient prerogatives of the King was the right to appoint "a suitable clerk to hold a void or vacant benefice or Church living until a regular pastor might be appointed." In the case referred to, the King had conferred the living on the Bishop, to be held along with the Bishopric; and the right of presentation having been disputed, Colt and Glover brought action against the Bishop. The case, being of particular importance, was, on April 20, 1616, heard in the Exchequer Chamber, before all of the judges; Bacon, as Attorney-General arguing for the King, and the Lord Bishop of Winchester being present to make report of the proceedings. He represented to the King that the argument was not

[5] Colt and Glover v. Bishop of Coventry and Lichfield, Hobart's Reports, 140–166.

merely as to any informality in the particular grant, but concerned the right of the Crown to grant Commendams except in case of necessity. Serjeant Chibborne argued that there could be no such necessity to grant Commendams to Bishops "because there was no need of augmentation of livings, for no man was bound to keep hospitality above his means." The day appointed for the judges to deliver their opinions was April 27, 1616; but before this time the King directed Bacon to notify Coke not to proceed with the case until the King had been consulted. Bacon's letter to Coke was dated April 25, and upon its receipt Coke asked that similar letters be sent to the other judges. This was accordingly done. The judges, however, met on April 27, argued the case, and adjourned it until June 8. They then sent a letter to the King stating that the case was "between subjects;" that the express words of the judges' oaths were "that in case any letters come unto us contrary to law, that we do nothing by such letters but certify your Majesty thereof, and go forth to do the law, notwithstanding the same letters;" and that they held the letters of the Attorney-General "to be contrary to law, and such as we could not yield to the same by our oath." To this letter the King replied in writing as follows: "Our pleasure is . . . that you forbear to meddle any further in this plea till our coming to town, and that out of our own mouth you may hear our pleasure in this business."

So the matter rested until June, when on the sixth of the month a Privy Council meeting was held, all of the judges being present, that the King in person might declare his will and receive the submission of the judges. The date was chosen so that the hearing of the case set for June 8 might not be held. To prepare the King for this meeting, Bacon drew up an elaborate memorandum. The Council being convened, the King recited the events which have already been related, and ordered to be read the various letters that had been written. He then soundly berated the judges for their errors and omissions,—that they had permitted too free discussion of the King's prerogative, that they had disobeyed his commandments, and only after this disobedience, had notified him of their action. What then happened let the report of the Act of Council tell:[6]

"After this his Majesty's declaration, all the judges fell down upon their knees, and acknowledged their error for matter of form, humbly craving his Majesty's gracious favour and pardon for the same.

"But for the matter of the letter, the Lord Chief Justice of the King's Bench entered into a defence thereof . . ."

The King then answered Coke, and called upon the Lord Chancellor and Attorney-General Bacon to give their opinions, which they did, disagreeing with Coke.

"Thereupon his Majesty and the Lords thought good to ask the judges severally their opinion; the question being put in this manner: Whether, if at any time, in a case depending before the judges, which his Majesty conceived to concern him either in power or profit, and thereupon required to consult with them, and that they should stay proceedings in the meantime, they ought not to stay accordingly? They all (the Lord Chief Justice only except) yielded that they would, and acknowledged it to be their duty so to do; only the Lord Chief Justice of the King's Bench said for answer, that when that

[6] Bacon's Letters, Spedding ed. 5:365.

case should be, he would do that should be fit for a judge to do . . ."

The other outstanding episode is known as the Præmunire case. Præmunire is the first word of a writ which was issued in certain cases to warn the accused to appear and answer. The writ was first authorized under a Statute of 27 Edward 3, Chap. 1, which was directed against the exercise of jurisdiction in England by the Court of Rome. The statute enacted penalties against all subjects who should "draw any out of the realm in plea, whereof the cognizance pertaineth to the King's Court," and who should fail to appear before the King or one of his courts to answer for the contempt committed. The penalties of præmunire were subsequently applied to other offences of various kinds. When the Court of Chancery began to take jurisdiction of cases which had already been decided by the Court of King's Bench, Coke sought means of preventing what, to him, was an unwarranted interference with his power. He found authority for his position in the Statutes of 27 Edward 3, Chap. 1, and 4 Henry 4, Chap. 23, which, he contended, forbade all other courts from meddling with any case which the King's Bench had decided. Straightway, he put his theory into practice.

A man against whom a fraudulent creditor had obtained a judgment in the King's Bench, applied in vain to the same court for a reversal. He then carried his case into Chancery and there obtained a decree in his favor. For nonexecution of this decree, the fraudulent creditor was sent to prison. The case thereupon came again before the King's Bench on application for a writ of habeas corpus. Coke decided that the decree and imprisonment, being after a judgment at Common Law, were unlawful, and that the prisoner ought to be released. But Coke did not stop here. He carried the contest into the enemy's camp by declaring that the granting of the decree in Chancery was an indictable offense. Therefore, on February 12, 1615, indictments of præmunire were preferred in the King's Bench against all persons who had been concerned in the proceedings in Chancery,—plaintiff, counselors, solicitors and clerks. The indictments failed only because the Grand Jury could not be induced to find a true bill.[7] The whole proceeding being reported by Bacon, Attorney-General, to the King, James appointed a committee of the Privy Council to examine the precedents and make recommendations to him. The report was adverse to Coke's contentions, and the King, therefore, on July 18, 1616, issued a "decree touching the granting of Præmunires against any for suing in Chancery after a judgment at Common Law," which commanded "that our Chancellor or Keeper of the Great Seal for the time being shall not hereafter desist to give unto our subjects upon their several complaints now or hereafter to be made such relief in Equity (notwithstanding any former proceedings at the Common Law against them) as shall stand with the true merits and justice of their cases, and with the former ancient and continued practice and precedency of our Chancery." [8]

In both the Commendams case and the Præmunire case, Coke had brought himself into conflict with the King, and had laid himself open to attack by Bacon. In both he suffered defeat, though carrying himself with boldness and dignity which have excited much admiration. He was, however, riding for a fall. Even before

[7] Courtney v. Glanvil, Cro. Jac. 343.
[8] Bacon's Letters, Spedding ed. 5:395.

the issuance of the above decree he had been called before the Privy Council on charges preferred by the Solicitor General, Sir Henry Yelverton. This was on June 26, 1616. To complaint of Coke's conduct in the Commendams and Præmunire cases, were added charges of complicity in pecuniary transactions of a doubtful character. Coke's answers were unsatisfactory, and when the whole proceeding was reported to the King, the latter decided upon further action. In the meantime, incited by the character of the rulings that Coke had been making from the bench, an investigation had been made into the doctrines contained in his Reports. Therefore, when on June 30, 1616, Coke was again called before the Council, he was informed by the King's command that he was temporarily suspended from the exercise of his duties as Privy Councilor and from judicial duties on the bench. His leisure was to be employed in reviewing and correcting his Reports. "And having corrected what in his discretion he found meet in those Reports, his Majesty's pleasure was that he should bring the same privately to himself, that he might consider thereof, as in his princely judgment should be found expedient."

Serious as the situation now was for Coke, he might easily have extricated himself from it, if he had been willing to unbend somewhat, and play the courtier's part. The King evidently wished to deal gently with Coke, while the King's favorites feared him for his power, and respected him for his wisdom. He was wealthy, generally acknowledged as the oracle of the law, and possessed of many state secrets. If, in the matter of appointments to office, and in lip service to the King, he had now proved tractable, the whole matter of the Reports would doubtless have been dropped. But he did not take this course; and made no report to the King. Therefore, the latter directed Chancellor Egerton and Attorney-General Bacon to call Coke before the Council. Nothing satisfactory came of this meeting of October 2, 1616. Coke had found nothing of consequence to correct in his Reports. He said "that there were of his Reports eleven books, that contained about five hundred cases: that heretofore in other Reports, as namely those of Mr. Plowden (which he reverenced much) there hath been found nevertheless errors which the wisdom of time had discovered and later judgments controlled," and, wrote Egerton and Bacon to the King, "he enumerated to us four cases in Plowden which were erroneous; and thereupon delivered in to us the inclosed paper, wherein your Majesty may perceive that my Lord is an happy man, that there should be no more errors in his five hundred cases than in a few cases of Plowden." [9]

How now to deal with Coke? Bacon advised that the whole matter of the Reports be aired before the Council, but to this plan the King would not consent. At each stage of the proceedings he seemed reluctant to take the next step. Coke's opponents therefore prepared elaborate statements of the faults of Coke's Reports, and presented them to the King to stimulate him to action. One such statement, prepared by Egerton, goes into considerable detail. It was printed about the year 1710 by George Paul, who supplied a preface.[10] Just when it

[9] Bacon: Letters, Spedding ed., 6:94–96.

[10] The Lord Chancellor Egerton's Observations on the Lord Coke's Reports: particularly in the debate of causes relating to the Right of the Church; the Power of the King's Prerogative; the Jurisdiction of Courts; or, the Interest of the Subject. London, Printed by John Nutt . . . for Bernard Lintott . . . 4°. 2 p. l., iv, 22 + 2 p.

was written, whether before or after Coke's removal from the Bench, we do not know; but it well represents the charges that were made against him. "It is to be observed throughout all his Books," says Egerton, "that he hath as it were purposely laboured to derogate much from the rights of the Church, and dignity of churchmen, and to disesteem and weaken the power of the King in the ancient use of his Prerogative." Sometimes he reports the cases erroneously, sometimes gives decisions that were never made, and in most cases scatters in his own conceits. After these general statements, Egerton gives, as "a taste," examples of about thirty errors.

Such evidences as these prevailed upon his Majesty, and so, on October 17, 1616, Coke was called before Egerton, Bacon, and Yelverton, the Solicitor-General, and informed that the King "out of his gracious favour was pleased that his memory should be refreshed," since Coke had not made satisfactory answer, "and that he should be put in mind of some passages dispersed in his books, which his Majesty being made acquainted with did as yet distaste, until he heard his explanation and judgment concerning the same." A selection of five cases was made and the objectionable passages in them pointed out. Coke undertook to explain them all "in such sort that no shadow should remain against his Majesty's prerogative." On October 21, he returned his answer denying the interpretation that had been put upon his statements of the cases. Thus he remained recalcitrant, leaving the King and his advisers in a position from which they could not with dignity withdraw. Therefore, without pursuing the investigation of the Reports further, the King, on November 10, 1616, declared to the Council his intention of removing Coke from the

Bench. In his speech, says Chamberlain,[11] he used Coke with respect, and "gave him this character, that he thought him no way corrupt, but a good justicer; with so many other good words, as if he meant to hang him with a silken halter." This was not in the spirit of a speech which Bacon had prepared for the King in which he was to have said that he had given Coke the summer's vacation "to reform his Reports, wherein there be many dangerous conceits of his own uttered for law, to the prejudice of his Crown, Parliament, and subjects; . . . but that his Majesty hath failed of the redemption he desired, but hath met with another kind of redemption from him, which he little expected. For as to his Reports, after three months' time and consideration, he had offered his Majesty only five animadversions, being rather a scorn than a satisfaction to his Majesty." Bacon, however, had the satisfaction of preparing and sending to the King, on November 13, 1616, the order for Coke's removal, and the warrant for the appointment of Sir Henry Montague as his successor. In administering the oath of office to Montague, on November 15, the Lord Chancellor Egerton accused Coke "of many errors and vanities for his ambitious popularity." The current explanation of Coke's fall was that "four P's have overthrown and put him down,—that is Pride, Prohibitions, Præmunire, and Prerogative." [12]

The inquisition into the Reports was not yet at an end. On November 21, Bacon prepared for the King a warrant for reviewing them, and on November 24, a "Commission to Sir Henry Montague, Knight, and others, for

[11] Statham: Jacobean Letter-writer, p. 152.
[12] *Ibid.*, p. 151.

reviewing and reforming Sir Edward Coke's Reports" was issued.[13] The task of the appointees was not simple. In itself it was difficult, and moreover, Coke soon began to regain the Royal favor. This was partly due to the desire of Sir John Villiers, eldest brother of the Duke of Buckingham, to marry Coke's daughter, Frances. This alliance was urged by Buckingham, and opposed by Bacon; and Coke at first refused his consent on account of the enormous marriage portion that was demanded. This was the marriage about which were enacted the disgraceful scenes between himself and his wife, Lady Hatton. The marriage finally took place, and straightway, in September, 1617, Coke was recalled to the Council table. In the preceding March, Bacon had succeeded Egerton as head of the Court of Chancery, and he now saw to it that the Commission to review the Reports was enlarged. To this move, Coke replied by demanding a full investigation. His method was to address the King through the Duke of Buckingham, now his brother-in-law. This is the letter, written in October or November, 1617:—

"Above a year past, in my late Lord Chancellor's time, information was given to his Majesty that I, having published, in eleven works or books of reports, containing above six hundred cases, one with another, had written many things against his Majesty's prerogative. And I being by his Majesty's gracious favor called thereunto, all the exceptions that could be taken to so many cases in so many books fell to five, and the most of them, too, were by passages in general words; all which I offered to explain in such sort as no shadow should remain against his Majesty's prerogative, as in truth there did

[13] Dugdale: Origines Juridiciales, 1680, p. 62.

not; which, whether it were related to his Majesty, I know not. But thereupon the matter has slept all this time; and now the matter, after this ever-blessed marriage, is revived, and two judges are called by my Lord Keeper to the former that were named. My humble suit to your Lordship is, that if his Majesty shall not be satisfied with my former offer, viz., by advice of the judges to explain and publish, as is aforesaid, those five points, so as no shadow may remain against his prerogative, that then all the judges of England may be called hereunto. That they may certify also what cases I have published for his Majesty's prerogative and benefit, for the good of the Church, and quieting of men's inheritances, and good of the Commonwealth; for which purpose I have drawn a minute of a letter to the judges, which I assure myself your Lordship will judge reasonable." [14]

The exposition of both the merits and demerits of the Reports, called for by Coke, was never made. The Reports were never revised, "reformed" or corrected. As a political issue, the controversy was at an end. But this was not the end of Coke's career either as a law writer or as a political figure. That is a story, however, which must be separately told (Chapter IV.); while the remainder of this sketch must proceed with the account of the Reports themselves.

The Reports

It is certainly true, as remarked by Marvin,[15] that "no reports have passed through such an ordeal as Coke's." That they survived is in itself an indication of their in-

[14] Wallace: The Reporters, pp. 181–182.
[15] Legal Bibliography, p. 210.

herent worth. Even while they were undergoing the bitter attacks of Egerton, Yelverton and Bacon, the latter was forced to do them honor. In a long letter written by him in 1616 to James I., "touching the compiling and amendment of the laws of England" [16] he says "that (to give every man his due) had it not been for Sir Edward Coke's Reports (which though they may have errors, and some peremptory and extrajudicial resolutions more than are warranted, yet they contain infinite good decisions and rulings over of cases), the law by this time had been almost like a ship without ballast; for that the cases of modern experience are fled from those that are adjudged and ruled in former time." "And I do assure your Majesty," runs an ungracious compliment later on in the same letter, "I am in good hope, that when Sir Edward Coke's Reports and my Rules and Decisions shall come to posterity, there will be (whatsoever is now thought) question who was the greater lawyer." In this hope, Bacon was not justified. Coke was undoubtedly the better lawyer, while Bacon's fame rests on other accomplishments. The Reports are indeed foundations of our law, and retain an unrivaled position among the older legal publications. For modern purposes also they are still useful, and although many of the cases in them have become obsolete, yet many of them are to-day studied in the law schools and referred to as authority by counsel and judges in the courts.

Two editions in eleven parts were published in Coke's lifetime, and ten editions have since been issued. The last was in 1826. It contains thirteen parts in six volumes. The twelfth and thirteenth parts were first pub-

[16] Bacon: Letters, Spedding ed. 6: 61–71.

lished in 1656 and 1659 respectively. The manuscript of them was among the papers seized by Royal order at the time of Coke's death, and although most of the papers were restored to the heirs in 1641, these parts remained unpublished until the above dates. Neither of them is comparable either in substance or manner with those which were issued under Coke's personal direction.

There can be no question that Coke's Reports contained the most important cases decided in the long period covered by them; but, as has been seen, there has been much dispute over his method of reporting these cases. For each important case he gives, first, a verbatim copy of the pleadings; second, the facts of the case; third, the points of law involved; fourth, the arguments of counsel *pro* and *contra;* fifth, the opinions of the judges; and sixth, the decision. This plan seems to be systematic and comprehensive; but it became complicated because Coke's own ideas were interspersed by him among the statements of the lawyers and judges. In many instances it is impossible to disentangle Coke from the men whom he purports to report. He turned every judgment into a set of general propositions, which give the cases an appearance of great learning, but the learning of a treatise instead of a report.

Not the least interesting part of the Reports is the series of prefaces. They are unique in the history of law reports not only on account of their length, their number and the period of time covered by them, but also because of their character. If separated from the cases and collected by themselves the eleven prefaces written by Coke would form a substantial octavo volume of 239 pages. From the first to the last they cover a period of legal writing of fifteen years. They were written and published by Coke in parallel columns of Latin and English. It does not appear in which language he first wrote them, for both versions are to be found in the first editions of the various parts, and we may, therefore, assume that both are equally authoritative. They contain not only such material as is ordinarily found in a preface,—the reasons which had moved him to publish the Reports (some of which have already been quoted in this chapter); justification for the selection of cases and some discussion of them; his method of reporting; some biographical allusions;—but also elaborate treatment of other topics which commonly would be found in a treatise or in a work of legal history. The chief of these topics are: Advice as to the method of studying law; the course of study provided by the Inns of Court; the great books with which every student should be conversant; and the antiquity of the Common Law, the courts and the legal institutions of England. Space will not here permit a discussion of these topics in detail. Each of them is a study by itself, and each can be treated only by gathering together from all of the prefaces the allusions to the respective topics. Many of Coke's facts have been disputed, and we have seen that advocates of John Cowell [17] thought Coke to be no good historian; but we are all indebted to him for having shown an interest in, and recorded his opinions on, subjects of research which have been the study of eminent modern legal writers. As in the law itself, so in the study of its foundations and institutions, we find Coke a convenient and helpful starting point. He serves as a connecting link between the ancient and the modern in legal thought. His observations did not in his own time go unquestioned,

[17] See Chapter II.

and we, therefore, find him in his successive "editions" answering questions that had been raised, fortifying by authorities his previous assertions, and expanding thoughts which had been only mentioned or slightly developed.

The Reports in Verse

One of the strangest evidences of the popularity of Coke's Reports is that a serious attempt was made to transcribe them into verse. When I say that a serious attempt was made, I mean that some unknown versifier tried to compress the gist of the cases in the eleven parts of the Reports into a series of couplets (occasionally a quatrain); and there is no evidence that the task was approached in a flippant, playful or unlawyerlike spirit. The work was done as an aid to the student, and the book was issued with that intent. It was published in 1742 by J. Worrall, one of the most reputable of the publishers of the time and a legal bibliographer of note.[18] It is provided with a table of cases, a subject index, and references to the various previous editions of the Reports. When the verses were written we do not know. "An ancient manuscript of the following verses falling accidentally into my hands, in which no small pains must have been taken," says Worrall in the preface, "the publication thereof needs little apology, when it is considered these lines may at the same time not only refresh the memory, and instruct, but also afford a pleasing recreation to gentlemen of the law, and others, by shewing them in a narrow compass a copious and learned body of the law, supported with the authority of no less per-

[18] A second edition was published in 1825, and a third in 1826.

son than the great Sir Edward Coke, whose name so long as laws endure will probably be esteemed and revered for his great knowledge, penetrating judgment, and fine reasoning therein."

The author of the ancient manuscript was no poet, but he was something of a lawyer, and his experience in this attempt would have qualified him to write modern digest paragraphs and headnotes of cases. Think of compressing Shelley's case into two lines. Here is the result:—

"SHELLEY, Where ancestors a freehold take:
The words (*his heirs*) a limitation make."

The following are a few other cases taken at random:—

"SNAG, If a person says he kill'd my wife,
No action lies, if she be yet alive."

"HUME, In murder must the indictment lie
Exactly at the place where he did die."

"CAUDREY, 'Gainst common prayer if parson say
In sermon ought, bishop deprive him may."

"BURY, Divorce for his frigidity,
Issue by second wife shall lawful be."

"BOULSTON, If neighbour coney-boroughs make,
The conies I, in my own ground, may take."

"SIX CARPENTERS, Where the law entry gives,
T'abuse it, trespass *ab initio* is."

"MONOPOLIES, Granted by king are void,
They spoil the trade in which the youth's imploy'd."

Sir Thomas Littleton

CHAPTER IV

LITTLETON AND COKE UPON LITTLETON

"Glanville, Bracton, Littleton, Coke, Blackstone: these are the five masters," says Wambaugh in his introduction to Littleton's Tenures. Whether or not we accept this selection as final, there can be no doubt about the influence which these men had on the development of Anglo-American law, and none as to the greatness of the two who are the subject of the present chapter,—Littleton and Coke. They were separated in point of time by less than a century, yet Littleton stands at the end of the ancient period of English law and Coke at the beginning of the modern period. The hiatus between the general legal thought of Littleton's time and of Coke's is wide, but that between Littleton and Coke is short because the former was the most advanced writer of the 15th century, while Coke, himself a forward-looking man, always also looked back to the origins of things; and thus the chasm was bridged.

We have seen how great a figure Coke cut in a time when it was necessary to be a tower of strength to rise above the level of mediocrity. If Coke had never written a book he would have had his place in history. Littleton also was a man of affairs who lived not without honor in his own country and generation. His father was Thomas Westcote, a "King's servant in court," and his mother, Elizabeth de Littleton. As heir to his mother's large estates, the son took her name. Few details of Littleton's life are known, and few are needed for our purposes at this time. He was born about the year 1422, the exact date being uncertain. The record is almost a complete blank until he became a member of the Inner Temple, where later he was appointed reader. His first public office was that of Undersheriff of Worcestershire, to which he was appointed in 1447. From that time on his progress was rapid, as the chronology will show:—Recorder of Coventry, 1450; Serjeant-at-law, 1453; King's serjeant, 1455; Commissioner of Array for Warwickshire, Steward of the Marshalsea Court and Justice of the County Palatinate of Lancaster, 1456; Justice of the Common Pleas, 1466; Knight of the Bath, 1475. He died on August 23, 1481, and lies buried in Worcester Cathedral. The span of his life covered therefore the reigns of both Henry VI. (1422–1461) and Edward IV. (1461–1483), and he lived through the whole troubled period of the Wars of the Roses. Although he did not participate in these wars by taking arms, the general suspicion which rested upon any public man may account for the fact that twice he sought and obtained a general pardon—from Richard, Duke of York, in 1454, and from Edward IV., in 1461. The latter monarch showed him a special sign of favor when he made him Justice of the Common Pleas (April 27, 1466) by fixing his salary at 110 marks a year, "with an allowance of 106s. 11 1/3d. for a furred robe at Christmas and 66s. 6d. for a linen robe at Pentecost."

Littleton's career as a lawyer, public official and judge was undoubtedly eminent, but it may be questioned whether his renown would have reached to this day if it had been dependent on the outstanding events of his life. He would have disappeared in the limbo of time if it had not been for what must have been to him a minor and personal incident,—an incident the importance of which did not become evident until after his death. Littleton was married about the year 1444, and he had three sons, William, Richard and Thomas. All of them are mentioned in his will.[1] Two of these sons were lawyers. The youngest, Thomas, became Chief Justice of the Common Pleas and Lord Keeper. The second, Richard, was one of the Governors of the Inner Temple, in 1505. It is in connection with the education of this son that Littleton performed a service to the legal world which is of inestimable value and which has immortalized his name. For him he wrote a brief treatise on the Laws of England in relation to land,—the book now universally known as Littleton's Tenures. Lord Coke is authority for the statement that the book was written for the benefit of the son, Richard. Several times in the Tenures, Littleton addresses "my son" directly. An instance is in section 749:—"Now I have made to thee my sonne three books." Commenting on this section, Coke says:[2] "Here our author calleth . . . not only his sonne Richard, but every studient of the law to be accounted his sonne, and worthily, for that seeing our author had the honour to be in his time the Father of the law, and all good studients in the law justly account themselves the sons of the law . . . our author, as a carefull and prudent Father . . . gave excellent instructions in these his bookes both to his owne son, and to his adopted sons, to make them from age to age the more apt and able to understand the arguments and reasons of the law."

We do not know the date when the book was writ-

[1] Littleton's Tenures; Wambaugh ed. pp. xlvii-lvii.
[2] Coke upon Littleton, Section 749.

ten; but reasons for writing it appear when we recall that, up to the year of Littleton's death, no English law books had been printed. There were in existence numerous legal tracts, a few treatises and the volumes of Year Books, but all of these were in manuscript. The material for the study of the law must have been difficult of access and unsatisfactory when found. Littleton would be aware of this fact through his experience as student, lawyer and judge; and therefore, it is presumed, he sought to lessen the burden for his own son by setting down on paper a clear statement of one of the most difficult branches of the law. Wambaugh[8] points out Littleton's particular fitness for this task as shown by the fact that, early in his career when chosen reader to the Inner Temple, he selected as his subject the statute of Westminster II., *De donis conditionalibus,* which relates to estates tail. Nevertheless, Littleton was exceedingly modest about his work and in a famous Epilogue cautioned his son not to rely on it too slavishly. "And know, my son, that I would not have thee believe that all which I have said in these books is law, for I will not presume to take this upon me. But of those things that are not law, inquire and learn of my wise masters learned in the law." Then, to justify himself for setting down statements for which he could vouch only on information and belief, he says, "Notwithstanding albeit that certain things which are moved and specified in the said books are not altogether law, yet such things shall make thee more apt, and able to understand and apprehend the arguments and reasons of the law. For by the arguments and reasons in the law, a man more sooner shall come to the certainty and knowledge of the law."

[8] Tenures, p. xxviii.

Littleton had few models for a work on this particular topic. Some undoubtedly there were; for Littleton, referring to the first two parts of his work, says, "And these two little books I have made to thee for the better understanding of certain chapters of the Ancient Books of Tenures." One of these has come down to us under the title "The Old Tenures." It is of uncertain date, but conceded to have preceded Littleton. It is a mere tract of twenty-one pages, and may be seen in Coke's Law Tracts (London, 1764, pp. 305–326), and in the eleventh and twelfth editions of Coke on Littleton. Littleton did not however need a model. His work is a classic example of what can be accomplished when a well-informed person, with a definite purpose in mind, sets about the writing of a book with simplicity, bent only on the production of an accurate and lucid result. His purpose was to make clear to his son, without any show of learning, and untrammelled by "style," the difficulties of a well-defined portion of the law. The Old Tenures did however suggest the title by which Littleton's work, for distinguishment, was originally known, viz., the Tenores Novelli, or New Tenures.

About all that can be said with certainty of the date when the writing was done is that it was before the year 1480. If more information were known about the son Richard, some conjectures might be made. We can only guess that if Littleton was married in 1444, his second son might have been born in 1448, and that perhaps he was embarked on his legal studies eighteen years later, bringing us to the date 1466. It is possible, at least, that Littleton might have been writing for his son as early as this date. We know that the book existed in MS. in 1480, because a copy of it, still preserved in the library of the University of Cambridge, was bought in St. Paul's Churchyard, on July 27, 1480. (Wambaugh ed., p. lx.)

As we do not know the exact date when the book was written, so also we do not know precisely when it was first printed; but the date 1482 has quite generally been assigned to it. The doubt arises from the fact that the first five editions were issued without date. The first four editions had no title-pages. The evidence concerning the date of first printing is drawn from a study of the typography of the book, and from information as to the printers. The first edition was printed in London by Lettou and Machlinia as shown by the colophon; "Expliciût Tenores Novelli Impssi p. nos Iohez lettou & Willz de machlinia î Civitate Londonia juxta eccaz oim sco." The partnership between Lettou and Machlinia began about 1482, and ended in 1483, after which date the latter carried on the business alone. The printing office was situated "close to All Saints Church in the city." The copy of this edition in the British Museum Library is bound with the undated Abridgement des Statutes, printed by the same firm, probably about the same time. These two books share the honor of being the earliest law books printed in England,—which of them first came from the press we do not know. Littleton's book was, however, by far the more important, and we may be pardoned for hoping that it was actually the first. It was undoubtedly the first printed treatise on English law, and lacked only a few years of being the first English book printed on any subject. A perfect copy in the British Museum Library is described as a folio volume, with a printed page in size 4 13/16 x 7 5/8 inches. The type is a rough black letter resembling the formal manuscripts of the time, with illuminated letters at the beginning of the chapters. Many abbreviations are used. It begins with a table of contents divided into three books, numbered; and into chapters, unnumbered, with references to the folios as indicated by the signature marks. The language is Law French. The second edition to which the date 1483 is assigned was printed by Machlinia "in the opulent city of London near the bridge which is vulgarly called Flete Brigge;" and the third edition, which was the earliest known to Coke, was printed at Rouen, France, by William le Tailleur *"ad instantiam Richardi Pynson."* The first page contains the latter's monogram. Pynson, an apprentice to Caxton and an associate of Wynkyn de Worde, succeeded to Machlinia's business about 1490. "Soon after his commencement in business (say Ames and Herbert), he employed one William Tailleur, a printer of Roan, to print Littleton's Tenures, and some other law pieces for him; because, our laws being all made in the Norman French till the beginning of the reign of Henry VII., and the printers of that country understanding the language better, were certainly more capable of printing them correct. Afterwards, he, as well as others, had such helps, that the statutes and other law books were all printed at home."[4] Among the "other law pieces" printed by Tailleur was Statham's Abridgment, for which the same kind of type was used as for Littleton's Tenures. Since Statham's was the larger work, it is conjectured (Note to 11th ed. of Coke on Littleton) that "it was printed some time after the publication of Littleton's Tenures, and that Pynson's success in the lesser undertaking induced him to venture on the greater; which in those days was the work of two or three years."

[4] Ames-Herbert-Dibdin, Typographical Antiquities, 1812, 2: vi.

The first edition to contain both a date and a title-page was the sixth, the title being "Leteltun tenuris new correcte." Up to 1628, according to Wambaugh's lists, forty-two editions had been printed in Law French, and thirty-one editions had been printed in English,—seventy-three editions in all. After that date fourteen editions have thus far been published, one in Law French, two in Law French and modern French, nine in English, and two in Law French and English. This makes a total of eighty-seven editions of the original work, not counting for the present those by Coke. Up to the time of the death, about the year 1517, of Richard, the son for whom the book was written, six editions had appeared. Even this brave showing, in the infancy of law-book publishing, could not have foretold to Richard the great fortune which awaited the book. It was taken up by each of the successive law publishers of note, and, therefore, in the history of the art of printing, it is a landmark. Some of the publishers were Lettou and Machlinia, Pynson, Redman, Rastell (William and John), Berthelet, Middleton, Smyth, Wyer, Powell, Tottel, Petyt, Marshe, Yetswert (Charles and Jane), Wight, and the Company of Stationers. From the decrease in the number of editions after the year 1628 (fourteen) as compared with those before that date (seventy-three), it might fairly be assumed that the book, written early in the fifteenth century and published about 1482, had at last outlived its usefulness. Such an inference would, however, be incorrect, because in that very year the book was given new life as by the touch of a magic hand. In addition to the fourteen editions of Littleton's text alone, already mentioned as published since 1628, there have been twenty-five editions of Coke on Littleton. These stand in a group by themselves, but if considered as editions of Littleton bring the total up to 112.

We have seen (Chapter III.) that Coke, after his dismissal from the Lord Chief Justiceship of the King's Bench in 1616, gave up the writing of law reports and turned his mind to politics. He did not, however, withdraw his devotion from law, but prepared a work, no less important than his Reports, which was published in the year when his Parliamentary career ended, 1628. A perusal of the prefaces to his Reports will show how natural it was that this work should be a Commentary on Littleton's Tenures. In the third preface, he names Littleton as one of four books "most necessary and of greatest authority and excellency." In the tenth preface, after the lapse of twelve years, he further favorably characterizes the book as one "of sound and exquisite learning, comprehending much of the marrow of the Common Law." He then defends Littleton from the hostile criticism of Hottoman (De verbis feudalibus; see also Chapter II., where the bearing of Hottoman's comment on Cowell's fate is discussed), and ends with the following which seems to be the acme of praise:—"And for Littleton's Tenures I affirm and will maintain it against all opposites whatsoever, that it is a work of absolute perfection in its kind, and as free from error, as any book that I have known to be written of any human learning. And the posterity of this sage of the law (unto whom he is a great ornament) doth flourish unto this day, of whom a man of great excellency in his profession [Camden 574] hath justly said that he was a famous lawyer, etc., to whose Treatise of Tenures, saith he, the students of the Common Laws are no less beholding than the civilians to Justinian's Institutes." This opinion was published by Coke in 1613, fifteen years before the first edition of Coke on Littleton was issued. It does not require a wide stretch of the imagination to suppose that even in 1613, Coke had formed the idea that he would "maintain" the reputation of Littleton "against all opposites whatsoever" by issuing a definitive edition. At any rate, when Coke came to write the preface to his Commentary he remembered the words above quoted. "That which we have formerly written," he says, "that this book is the ornament of the Common Law, and the most perfect and absolute work that ever was written in any human science; and in another place, that which I affirmed and took upon me to maintain against all opposites whatsoever, that it is a work of as absolute perfection in its kind, and as free from error as any book that I have known to be written of any human learning, shall to the diligent and observing reader of these Institutes be made manifest, and we by them (which is but a Commentary upon him) be deemed to have fully satisfied that which we in former times have so confidently affirmed and assumed. His greatest commendation, because it is of greatest profit to us, is, that by this excellent work, which he had studiously learned of others, he faithfully taught all the professors of the law in succeeding ages. The victory is not great to overthrow his opposites, for there never was any learned man in the law, that understood our author, but concurred with me in this commendation. . . . Such as in words have endeavored to offer him disgrace, never understood him, and therefore we leave them in their ignorance, and wish that by these our labours they may know the truth and be converted. . . ."

Without this evidence that the study of Littleton by Coke was of long standing, and without taking into consideration the evidences of long and prodigious labors in the Commentary itself, it might safely have been assumed that throughout his legal career Littleton was his constant companion. Not only was it a sign of professional equipment to possess and refer to the Tenures, but the book was often printed on sheets with wide margins so that it might be used as a common place book for notes on the subject. For example, the editions of 1577, 1579, 1583, 1588, 1604 and 1612 were all so printed; and we learn from Johnson[5] that "there is in the library at Holkham an edition of Littleton's Tenures, in two volumes duodecimo, the margins of which are covered with the short referential notes of Sir Edward Coke, in his own handwriting, many of which the modern rebinder had mutilated." Certain it is that he set about doing justice to his favorite author, with no ordinary enthusiasm and devotion. This is shown in a special way by the fact that although Coke had set himself the task of preparing a general work in four volumes covering the chief features of English law to be known as the Institutes of the Laws of England, he did not endeavor to write a book on tenures which might supersede Littleton, but chose to make the first of his Institutes a volume which should do honor to Littleton. The title is "The First Part of the Institutes of the Lawes of England; or, a Commentarie upon Littleton, Not the name of a Lawyer onely, but of the Law Itselfe." In his preface he explains the plan of the great work of his old age (he was seventy-six in 1628). "This work," he says, "we have called, The First Part of the Institutes for two

[5] Life of Coke, 2:454.

causes: first, for that our author is the first book that our student taketh in hand: secondly, for that there are some other parts of Institutes not yet published, viz.: The second part, being a commentary upon the statute of Magna Charta, Westm. 1, and other old statutes. The third part treateth of criminal causes and pleas of the crown: which three parts we have by the goodness of Almighty God already finished. The fourth part we have purposed to be of the jurisdiction of courts: but hereof we have only collected some materials towards the raising of so great and honourable a building." He called his volumes Institutes, because his desire was that they "should institute and instruct the studious, and guide him in a ready way to the knowledge of the national laws of England."

The first edition of Coke on Littleton is a folio volume printed in London "for the Societie of Stationers, anno. 1628." The title-page is elaborately ornamented with columns, scrollwork, vases, fruit, flowers, birds, with a jewelled cartouche at the bottom. The frontispiece, which in the copy in the Columbia University Law Library precedes the title-page, is a kneeling figure of Littleton. Out of his mouth come the words "Ung Dieu e ung Roy," and underneath the portrait are the words, "The true portraiture of Judge Littleton the famous English lawyer." The preface by Coke is in English, with printed marginal references to authorities. It comprehends a brief account of Littleton's life and the facts about the writing and printing of the book as far as known to Coke. The general plan for the text requires three columns to the page, first, the original text in Law French; second, the English translation; and third, Coke's Commentary. There are also marginal references. The three-column arrangement, however, disappears whenever Coke's remarks outrun the original text. In fact, we may paraphrase Sheridan and say that there is often merely a neat rivulet of text running through a meadow of commentary. Thus, out of a very small volume, Coke made what he himself called a "painful and large volume," for which he apologetically accounts in the last sentence of his preface:—"Our labours herein are drawn out to this great volume, for that our author is twice repeated, once in French, and again in English." Three editions of Coke on Littleton were printed in Coke's lifetime. The second, with many corrections, was issued in 1629, and the third in 1633. The second edition contains a portrait of Coke, as well as the portrait of Littleton above described, which was prepared for this edition but is sometimes found inserted in the first edition. Since Coke's death, twenty-one editions have been published, the last being printed in Philadelphia, 1853.

The effect of adding Coke to Littleton was not merely to make a more bulky book. It was a virtual piling of Pelion on Ossa enabling the law student to scale the heights of legal learning. To use Wambaugh's phrase (Littleton, p. lxii.), the result is "the most conspicuous example of a masterpiece upon a masterpiece—much as if the plays of Shakespeare were entwined about the Canterbury Tales." It is true that there is a tradition that English lawyers read the whole of Littleton each Christmas day, a feat which could not be accomplished with Coke on Littleton; and it is true that Sir John Davies (Preface to his Reports) advocates the reading of the original work only. "The learned men in our law," said Davies, "have ever thought that Littleton, being a learned and reverend Judge, wrote with a purpose to be understood; and that therefore another man, especially if he were of less learning than he, could hardly express him better than he hath expressed himself. And therefore his Book hath ever been read of our youngest students without any Commentary or Interpretation at all." This must have been written before 1612 when Davies died, and therefore was not directed against Coke. There were in fact no printed commentaries on Littleton at that time, although there must have been many MS. comments in private hands. One such, which is said to antedate Coke's, was printed in 1829 by Henry Cary.[6]

There is no doubt, however, that Coke enhanced the value of Littleton, and as said by Charles Butler (Preface to 13th ed. of Coke on Littleton), the reputation of the Commentary "is not inferior to that of the work which is the subject of it." "The most proper point of view in which the merit and ability of Sir Edward Coke's writings can be placed, is by considering him as the centre of modern and ancient law. . . . [The Commentary] is an immense repository of everything that is most interesting or useful in the legal learning of ancient times. . . . But his writings are not only a repository of ancient learning; they also contain the outlines of the principal doctrines of modern law and equity. . . . Thus his writings stand between, and connect the ancient and modern parts of the law, and by showing their mutual relation and dependency, discover the many ways

[6] A Commentary on the Tenures of Littleton; written prior to the publication of Coke upon Littleton. Edited from a copy in the Harleian collection of manuscripts by Henry Cary, Esq., Barrister-at-Law, of Lincoln's Inn. London, 1829. For an account of this publication, see Seymour, Charles B.; Coke's Reports, and the anonymous Commentary on Littleton, *Law Library Journal,* 10: 1–2.

by which they resolve into, explain, and illustrate one another." The work of these two men, combined into a "painful volume," has become a symbol for all books which, sparing neither author nor reader in going to the bottom of things, say the last words on the subjects of which they treat. A recognition of this reputation is found in Sir Walter Scott's novel "The Antiquary" (chapter 35). Mr. Blattergowl, the preacher, excusing the Antiquary's sister, that she may prepare the supper, says to her: "I can amuse myself very weel with the larger copy of Erskine's Institutes." "And," says Scott, "taking down from the window seat that amusing folio (the Scottish Coke upon Littleton), he opened it, as if instinctively, at the tenth title of Book Second, 'Of Teinds, or Tythes,' and was presently deeply wrapped up in an abstruse discussion concerning the temporality of benefices."

The account of Lord Coke's Reports (Chapter III.) brought the story of his life down to the year 1620, when he was elected member of Parliament for Liskeard. Immediately, he became a leader and an advocate of the "liberties of Parliament." Thus he incurred the disfavor of James I., and at the dissolution of Parliament, he, with other leaders, was arrested and confined in the Tower for nine months. In August, 1622, he was released on condition that he remain within certain limits. Before the death of James (March 27, 1625), Coke was back in the House of Commons, and he sat in both the first and second Parliaments of Charles I. In 1628 he was returned for the last time, and made his last great speech. In spite of the King's prohibition, he spoke boldly against the Duke of Buckingham. To the very end of his life he was a vigorous old man, riding horseback regularly at eighty. And he was a figure to be reckoned with in party strife because of his great knowledge both of the law and of events and people. That he was held both in fear and reverence is shown by the reply of Sir John Walter, Lord Chief Baron of the Exchequer, in 1630, when a brief was sent him against Coke. "Let my tongue cleave to the roof of my mouth," he said, "when I open it against Sir Edward Coke." Coke had at that time already published his First Institute, and as we have seen prepared the second and third volumes. These dealt with matters which touched the King's prerogative, and Charles was fearful of the effect of their publication. This is shown by a letter written at his direction, January 24, 1631,[7] by Henry Earl of Holland, to Secretary Dorchester.

"I am commanded by his Majesty to tell you that you must send to my Lord Keeper about a book that Sir Edward Coke is setting forth, in the which the King fears somewhat may be to the prejudice of his prerogative, for he is held too great an oracle amongst the people, and they may be misled by anything that carries such an authority as all things doth that he either speaks or writes, for the prevention of which the King thinks it fit it should not come forth. His Majesty hears that Sir Edward Coke, though he be in no present danger, yet, they say, through a late indisposition he is not likely to last long. He would have you choose some person that you may trust to inquire after his health, and, if he be in any present danger, that care may be taken to seal up his study, if he dies, where such papers are as use may be made of them (having passed through so many

[7] Calendar of State Papers. Domestic Series, 1629–1631, p. xxvi.

great places in the State), for his Majesty's service, and some suppressed that may disserve him."

Coke was indeed ill, but not in immediate danger. His complaint was old age, a disease which he himself said "all the drugs of Asia, the gold of Africa, the silver of America, nor all the doctors of Europe could cure." The design to sequester his papers was however kept in mind; and on July 24, 1634, the King ordered Secretary Windebank "to repair to his [Coke's] house, and there to seize, take into his charge, and bring away all such papers and manuscripts as he shall think fit, and all Justices of Peace and other the King's officers are to be assisting to him in the performance of that service." [8] The order was not immediately executed, but in August, Coke's study in the Inner Temple was sealed up. On September 3, 1634, Coke died. When he was on his deathbed, according to Roger Coke,[9] "Sir Francis Windebank, Laud's old friend, by an Order of Council came to search for seditious and dangerous papers; by virtue whereof, he took Sir Edward Coke's Comment upon Littleton, and the history of his life before it, written with his own hand, his Comment upon Magna Charta, etc., the Pleas of the Crown, and Jurisdiction of Courts, and his 11th and 12th Reports in manuscript, and I think 51 other manuscripts, with the last will of Sir Edward, wherein he had for several years been making provisions for his younger grandchildren." On December 4, 1634, Windebank directed Nicholas to examine the papers in Coke's study in the Temple, and on the 9th, he further instructed him to deliver to Sir Robert Coke, Edward's heir, all

[8] Calendar of State Papers, Domestic Series, 1634–1635, p. 165.

[9] Detection of the Court and State of England, 2d ed. Book 2, p. 107.

papers which did not concern his Majesty's service. On the 10th, Nicholas delivered the retained papers to Windebank.

The papers remained in the possession of the King until 1641, and some of them were never given up. Roger Coke, continuing the above quotation, says "that the books and papers were kept till seven years after, when one of Sir Edward's sons in 1641 moved the House of Commons, that the books and papers taken by Sir Francis Windebank, might be delivered to Sir Robert Coke, heir of Sir Edward, which the King was pleased to grant, and such as could be found were delivered; but Sir Edward's will was never heard more of to this day." The Journals of the House of Commons (2:80 and 85) for February 6 and 13, 1640, give the basis for this statement. The record reads that, on the former date, "Sir Tho. Roe is desired from this House, to remember his Majesty of his gracious promise, concerning the books of Sir Edw. Coke; and to speak with the Lord Keeper, and the Lord Chief Justice of the Common Pleas, that some course may be taken for the discovery of them, where they are; and for the restoring of them to the executors of Sir Edw. Coke, according to former promise." On February 13, it was "ordered, that the several books of Sir Edw. Coke, deceased, which are now come to his executor's hands, be delivered to Sir Robert Coke, according to the intention of the said Sir Edw. Coke." Further action was taken in the following year (March 7, 1641, House Journals, 3:470) when it was "Resolved, upon the question, That it shall be referred to Mr. Bridgeman, Mr. Prideaux, and Mr. Hill, to draw a bill for the licensing of Sir Edward Coke's books; and for the preventing the reprinting of them, for a time certain, to be assigned in the bill." The bill above referred to may have been enacted, but it does not appear in Scobell's Acts of the Interregnum, although some acts of 1641 are included; nor in the Acts and Ordinances of the Interregnum (London, 1911) which begins with March 5, 1641/2. There was still hesitancy on the part of the Crown in deciding just what manuscripts should be delivered to the heir. That some papers were never returned and probably were destroyed appears from the fact that in November, 1642, Sir Francis Windebank "by the King's command" decided "to keep five manuscripts taken from Sir Edward Coke, of very great consideration."[10] We are certain, of course, that the Second, Third and Fourth of the Institutes, said by Roger Coke to have been among the manuscripts seized, and probably referred to as "Sir Edward Coke's books," in the House Resolution of March 7, 1641, were actually published; the Second in 1642, and the Third and Fourth in 1644. If Coke's Detection may be relied on, a fact doubted by many, the Third Institute played a part in political affairs even before it was published. He says[11] that after Charles had gone to York in 1642, and "before it came to sword and pistol, men began a war with their pens: And herein it is observable, that the writers for the King chiefly maintained his cause out of Sir Edward Coke's Pleas of the Crown, which by order of the King's council, was upon Sir Edward's deathbed, seized as dangerous and seditious; and I do not find any who wrote for the Parliament, ever used any one topick out of it to justifie their cause; tho' it and Sir Edward's

[10] Calendar of State Papers, Domestic Series: Charles I., 1641–43, p. 414.

[11] Detection, 2: 134–135.

other books of the Comment upon Magna Charta, and Jurisdiction of Courts, were printed by order of the House of Commons, and by them petitioned that the King would deliver the originals to Sir Robert Coke, Sir Edward's heir." [12] If the Pleas of the Crown was so used it is a curious reversal of the fate which Charles had prepared for the book when he sought to prevent its publication for fear that it might contain something to the prejudice of his prerogative. While speaking of this Third Institute it may be interesting to notice that Pepys in his Diary on November 15, 1667, after the beheading of Charles I. was long past, and Charles II. was on the throne, remarks that after some persuasion he got Mr. Moore "to read part of my Lord Coke's chapter on treason, which is mighty well worth reading, and do inform me in many things, and for aught I see, it is useful now to know what these crimes are." Also it may be noted in passing that the Fourth Institute was in 1669 violently assailed by William Prynne in a book entitled "Brief Animadversions on, Amendments of, and Additional Record to the Fourth Part of the Institutes." Prynne, with acrimonious pen, accused Coke of piracy, chiefly from Manwood's Treatise of the Forest Laws.

Of the personality of Littleton, we know nothing, and enthusiasm respecting him must be directed to his book. About Coke, on the contrary, there is a wealth of fact and anecdote. His chief characteristics were reverence for the learning of his profession, capacity for labor, ambition and the strength to fight for the goal of it. He seems to have merited and demanded respect for his

[12] The Third Institute, Pleas of the Crown, was not published until 1644 and therefore was available for quotation by only a limited number of people.

ability and scholarship, and to have been universally feared as well as respected. According to Roger Coke [13] it was his practice to work systematically, giving so much time to each of his vocations. He went to bed at nine o'clock and rose at three A. M.; during this period even a King's messenger was not allowed to disturb him. When this was attempted at one A. M. in connection with the warrant for the arrest of the Earl of Somerset, Coke's son answered: "If you come from ten kings, you shall not [see him]; for I know my father's disposition to be such, that if he be disturbed in his sleep, he will not be fit for any business."

There was not much softness about him. His controversy with his wife, and the manner in which he forced her daughter into a marriage of convenience, have given him the reputation of a hard-hearted man. His treatment of prisoners at the bar was crude and cruel. Nothing can be said to mitigate the brutality of his prosecution, while he was Attorney General, of Sir Walter Raleigh, on trial for his life. He was a man to be criticised only at one's peril—a stiff-necked man, who, as we have seen, found it impossible to bow the head even to the King in Council. This characteristic has become a tradition. When Samuel Johnson and Sir Alexander Macdonald, on March 27, 1772, were discussing the question whether "almost all great lawyers, such at least as have written upon law, have known only law, and nothing else," Johnson referred to Hale and Selden as examples of lawyers who knew and wrote about many other things. Sir Alexander countered with "Very true, Sir; and Lord Bacon. But was not Lord Coke a mere lawyer?" Johnson answered, "Why, I am afraid he

[13] Detection, 1: 49.

was; but he would have taken it very ill if you had told him so. He would have prosecuted you for scandal." [14]

On the other hand, Coke's books themselves offer much evidence that he was a man of deep religious feeling who, though regarding the Priesthood of Themis with veneration, felt himself called upon first of all to serve both God and Country. That he was a man of strong emotions is shown by an incident which Carlyle has made famous. When Charles I.'s third Parliament was nearing its close, the House was drawing up its Petition of Right, and many veiled speeches were made against the Duke of Buckingham. Then came a message from Charles requiring the members "not to cast or lay any aspersion upon any Minister of his Majesty." "Sir Robert Philips of Somersetshire spake, and mingled his words with weeping. Mr. Pym did the like. Sir Edward Coke, overcome with passion, seeing the desolation likely to ensue, was forced to sit down when he began to speak, by the abundance of tears." Later he controlled himself and for the first time in that Parliament named boldly "the author and cause of all those miseries"—the Duke of Buckingham. "Why did those old honourable gentlemen weep?" asks Carlyle. "How came tough old Coke upon Littleton, one of the toughest men ever made, to melt into tears like a girl, and sit down unable to speak? The modern honourable gentleman cannot tell. Let him consider it, and try if he can tell! And then . . . try if he can discover why he cannot tell!" [15] No one has attempted to answer Carlyle's rhetorical question, and perhaps such an answer could come only from

[14] Boswell's Johnson; Hill ed., 2: 158.

[15] Carlyle: Oliver Cromwell's Letters and Speeches. London, 1897, 1: 61–63.

Coke himself. Did he give it when, in the same year in which the above incident took place, he dedicated his First Institute as follows:—

"Deo, Patriæ, Tibi."

Is there not here shown a religious fervor, a patriotic devotion, a solicitude that the law be upheld, which might account for a public show of emotion when the State was in danger, followed by an attack on its enemy, regardless of personal consequences? He ends his book with the words:—

"And for a farewell to our Jurisprudent, I wish unto him the gladsome light of Jurisprudence, the lovelinesse of Temperance, the stability of Fortitude, and the soliditie of Justice."

CHAPTER V

Blackstone and His Commentaries

It is said that the fact that William Blackstone, at the age of twelve, was left an orphan, saved him from being a prosperous tradesman. Whether or not the conclusion is correct, the premise cannot be attacked, for he was the posthumous child of Charles Blackstone, "a silk-man, and a citizen and bowyer of London," and his mother died twelve years after his father. He was born on July 10, 1723, in Cheapside, in the parish of St. Michael le Querne, London. Had his father lived it is assumed that Blackstone also would have been a dealer in silk and a maker of bows for archers; but as matters fell out his education was taken under the care of his maternal uncle, Thomas Bigg, a surgeon of London. At the age of seven he was sent to the Charter-House School, where he made such progress that at fifteen (November 30, 1738) he entered Pembroke College, Oxford. He early showed an inclination for poetry, and took a prize for some verses on Milton. He does not appear to have planned especially to take up the study of law, and his years at Pembroke were devoted to the usual subjects. At one time he showed a fondness for architecture, and at the age of twenty wrote a treatise on the Elements of Architecture, which however was never published.

His legal career began when on November 20, 1741, he was admitted to the Middle Temple. He marked the change by writing a poem entitled "The Lawyer's Fare-

Sir William Blackstone

well to the Muse."[1] In it, he laments the fact, that, like an exile, he is now driven from his old haunts, to which he turns back a regretful eye. His description of what is before him was not reassuring:—

"Me wrangling courts and stubborn Law
To smoke and crowds and cities draw:
There selfish Faction rules the day,
And Pride and Av'rice throng the way;
Diseases taint the murky air,
And midnight conflagrations glare;
Loose Revelry and Riot bold
In frighted street their orgies hold;
Or when in silence all is drown'd,
Fell murder walks her lonely round;
No room for Peace, no more for you;
Adieu, celestial nymph, adieu!"

Nevertheless, in order to seek the "harmonious rule of right," he turns to his new calling with enthusiasm, asking only that his "setting sun" may find his honor and his conscience clear.

"Then welcome business, welcome strife,
Welcome the cares the thorns of life,
The visage wan, the pore-blind sight,
The toil by day, the lamp at night,
The tedious forms, the solemn prate,
The pert dispute, the dull debate,
The drowsy bench, the babbling Hall,—
For thee, fair Justice, welcome all."

As this was supposed to be Blackstone's farewell to poetry, let us now conclude that subject by noticing that in spite of his poem, he later wrote a number of verses

[1] Browne: Law and Lawyers in Literature, pp. 230–233.

including "The Lawyer's Prayer,[2] a poem on the death of Frederick, Prince of Wales[3] and some unpublished translations and juvenile pieces. A writer in the Dictionary of National Biography remarks that his verses were "full of the strained and stilted mannerisms of the period," and that English literature lost nothing when he entered the law. Be that as it may, one of the merits of his Commentaries is their literary style. He was a close student of Shakespeare and communicated annotations to Malone who used them in his Supplement to the edition of Shakespeare's Plays, published in 1778 by Samuel Johnson and George Steevens. Malone says,[4] "The notes which he gave me on Shakespeare show him to have been a man of excellent taste and accuracy, and a good critick."

Having been elected a fellow of the Society of All Souls College in 1743, he divided his time between the University and the Temple. He "commenced" Bachelor of Civil Law, June 12, 1745, and was called to the Bar, November 28, 1746. His connection with the University continued, and he held successively the offices of Bursar and Steward of the Manors. In 1749, he was elected Recorder of Wallingford, in succession to his uncle. In the next year he became Doctor of Civil Law, and published "An Essay on Collateral Consanguinity." This was written to assist All Souls College in determining the rights of kin of the founder to priority in election to the society. This work was Blackstone's first legal publication. He had been at the bar seven years, when he determined to give up the practice of the law and retire

[2] Browne: Law and Lawyers in Literature, p. 234.
[3] Gentleman's Magazine, 51: 335–336.
[4] Prior: Life of Malone, p. 431.

to his fellowship and lead an academic life. This he did in 1753, beginning immediately the preparation of a series of lectures on the laws of England.

Just at this time the Civil Law professorship at Oxford became vacant, and Mr. Murray (afterwards Lord Mansfield) urged the Chancellor, the Duke of Newcastle, to appoint Blackstone to the post. The interview at which Blackstone was introduced to the Duke, with a view to carrying out this project, is given by Holliday (Life of Mansfield, p. 89). "Sir," said the Duke, "I can rely on your friend Mr. Murray's judgment as to your giving law lectures in a good style, so as to benefit the students; and I dare say, that I may safely rely on you, whenever anything in the political hemisphere is agitated in that University, you will, sir, exert yourself in our behalf." The answer was, "Your Grace may be assured that I will discharge my duty in giving law lectures to the best of my poor abilities." "Aye! Aye!" replied his Grace hastily, "and your duty in the other branch too." Unfortunately for the new candidate, says Holliday, he only bowed assent; and a few days afterwards he had the mortification to hear that Dr. Jenner, the Duke's original candidate, had been appointed. Under these circumstances, and on the advice of Murray, Blackstone then determined to read his lectures at the University to such listeners as he could get. He was immediately successful. In the next year, 1754, as an aid to his hearers, he published "An Analysis of the Laws of England." This, and his lectures, were the basis for his Commentaries. In the preface to volume one of the latter, he says: "The following sheets contain the substance of a course of lectures on the laws of England, which were read by the author in the University of Oxford. His original plan took its rise in the year 1753; and, notwithstanding the novelty of such an attempt in this age and country, and the prejudices usually conceived against any innovations in the established mode of education, he had the satisfaction to find (and he acknowledges it with a mixture of pride and gratitude) that his endeavors were encouraged and patronized by those, both in the University and out of it, whose good opinion and esteem he was principally desirous to obtain." These lectures, not prescribed by the University, and drawing an audience by their own merit, were continued until 1758, when Blackstone was appointed first professor of law under the foundation established at Oxford by the will of Charles Viner, who had died in 1756.

Viner's Abridgment

Since the world is indebted to Viner for establishing the professorship under which Blackstone continued the preparation of his lectures and his Commentaries, and since Viner himself compiled the "most voluminous production of any single individual in the whole bibliography of the common law," a work directly connected with Blackstone's professorship, it is appropriate to pause in our narrative to give him credit and to describe the circumstances which led up to his gift. Charles Viner was born in 1678 and matriculated at Oxford in 1694. Later, he had chambers in the Temple (King's Bench Walk), but he was never called to the Bar. For many years he lived on his estate at Aldershot in Hampshire. He devoted nearly fifty years of his life to the compilation of a General Abridgment of Law and Equity, which he published at his own expense on paper specially manufactured, and bearing the watermark "C. V." The volumes bear the imprint, Aldershot in Hampshire, but this is the only evidence that they were actually printed there. Only one edition was published during his lifetime. It consists of twenty-three volumes, folio, and the period of issuance extended from 1742 to 1753. In the preface to volume one, he says that he had never entertained any thoughts of making his own work public, designing it merely to supplement for his own use the Abridgments of Rolle, Danvers and Nelson. "The commencement of this work," he says, "was with the present century, at which time I was admitted a member of the Honourable Society of the Middle Temple, and attended, as a student, the courts of Westminster. After the coming out of the first volume of Mr. Danvers' Abridgment (that most curious and exact work) I began to slacken in proceeding with my own, and being under some apprehensions of having injured my health by a very close application, I retired into the country, and for some years wholly laid aside prosecuting my undertaking without intermedling with business of law, unless in preventing and compromising differences among neighbors, and others applying to me, at some expence to myself but none to them." He then began to revise the work that he had already done, by comparison with the Abridgments of Nelson, Danvers, Hughes and Shephard, and finding them for the most part copyists of each other, and inaccurate, he determined to complete his own Abridgment, beginning however where Danvers had left off (viz., the title Error), and to publish it for the benefit of students. "The study of the law," he wrote, "is a very long journey, and the roads not the plainest, in which they [Abridgments] may serve as posts and

Mercuries to direct the students in their way, but ought not by any means to be considered as their journey's end, or place of their last resort and residence." His frank criticism of the works of others, and the method by which he published his own, roused the opposition of booksellers and publishers, and the University of Cambridge which claimed the monopoly of law-book publishing. In his various prefaces he complains bitterly of the difficulties that were put in his way and the failure of subscribers to redeem their pledges. Nevertheless he persevered with his project, declaring that "be my fate what it will, should it prove like that of the Tarpeian maid, to be oppressed with my own volumes, as she was with the helmets of the Sabines, yet it would be some consolation that it could reflect no dishonor upon me, whatever it might upon others." When he had issued the volumes from the word Factor to Y, he determined to complete the alphabet by adding the titles from A–Ex. Thus volume 1 of the first edition begins with E and volume 11 with A.

Of the Abridgment, Justice Story wrote in 1835, "its principal merit is its extent; and though in some points it is redundant, in others defective, and in all irregular, it is a vast index of the law, which time and patience can master, and it often rewards the labor when all other resources have failed." A less favorable comment is that "it is a vast and labyrinthine encyclopædia of legal lore ill arranged and worse digested. Valueless as an authority, it was but an indifferent help to research until the publication of Kelham's Index." It has in truth long since passed from use, but was, even during the course of publication, destined by the author for a beneficent end. In the preface to volume six, after thanking those who had praised his work and sharply berating those who opposed it, he says that he is little concerned with the great expense to which the publication has put him, being satisfied with the honor that attaches to the attempt. "If anyone yet doubts the reality of these professions," he says, "let him at least suspend judgment for a time, and if he sees this work dedicated (in such manner, as I shall be advised) to the perpetual service of my country, and benefit of posterity, it may be hoped that then at least he will be undeceived. At least I shall have the satisfaction of disappointing a set of men, who so far from endeavoring to serve their country, act as if they looked on all authors as their prey." This was published in 1743. His work was not complete until 1753, and he died on June 5, 1756. Then it became known that on December 20, 1755, he had made a will leaving to Oxford University the copyright and all of the remainder copies of his Abridgment, and his residuary real and personal property, amounting in all to about £12,000, in trust to establish a professorship of the Common Law and to endow fellowships and scholarships in the same subject. For this gift Viner was enrolled among the public benefactors of the University by decree of the Convocation. Blackstone remarks in volume one of his Commentaries (p. 28) that appreciation was further shown by the "alacrity and unexampled dispatch" with which the University put into effect the terms of the bequest, and by the regulations made to guard the benefaction from neglect and abuse. Within a year and a half the administrators with the will annexed (Drs. West and Good of Magdalene, Dr. Whalley of Oriel, Mr. Buckler of All Souls, and Mr. Betts of University College) had collected and settled

Viner's effects, had printed "near a volume of his work," and disposed of nearly the whole of it, and had made up the accounts. Another six months they spent in planning for the professorship and in drawing up the statutes, which were confirmed by Convocation on July 3, 1758.

From the above wording, it would appear that some part of the Abridgment needed reprinting by the University in order that complete sets of it might be sold. At any rate we know from the preface to the second edition that complete sets of the first were scarce and expensive, and that for some time the University intended to issue the second edition in order to increase the returns from the Vinerian fund. This project appearing impractical, "as incompatible with the state of the Vinerian fund," the University and the Clarendon Press entered into an arrangement with Robinson, Payne and others to issue the new edition. This was done in twenty-four volumes, octavo, 1791–1794, with a supplement of six volumes, 1799–1806.

The Vinerian Professorship

The statutes relative to the professorship made in accordance with the will, as given by Blackstone (Commentaries, 1:28n), are worthy of notice as a step in the development of legal education. The professor, who must be at least a Master of Arts or a Bachelor of Civil Law of Oxford of ten years' standing, was to be elected by Convocation. The salary was two hundred pounds a year. He must either by himself or by approved deputy "read one solemn public lecture on the laws of England, and in the English language, in every academical term, . . . or forfeit twenty pounds for every omission to

Mr. Viner's general fund," and he must each year in person or by deputy "read one complete course of lectures on the laws of England, and in the English language, consisting of sixty lectures at the least; to be read during the University term time, with such proper intervals that not more than four lectures may fall within any single week." The course must be given *gratis* to the scholars of Mr. Viner's foundation, but a fee, the amount of which was to be settled by Convocation, might be demanded of other auditors. The fee later determined upon was four guineas for the first course, and two for the second course. For every one of the said sixty lectures omitted, the professor, on complaint made to the Vice-Chancellor within the year, "must forfeit forty shillings to Mr. Viner's general fund." The professorship was for life, during good behavior. Fellowships with an annual stipend of forty pounds, and scholarships of thirty pounds were also created. This professorship is still in existence, known as the Vinerian Professorship of Common Law, and still supported in part by the proceeds of the Vinerian foundation.

The first professor, elected on October 20, 1758, was William Blackstone, who in the intervening period from 1753 had been reading lectures as already related. His first lecture as Vinerian professor was read on October 25th. In the same year this lecture was published at the request of the Vice-Chancellor and Heads of Houses, and subsequently served as the introduction to the Commentaries. The spirit in which Blackstone undertook his new duties, and the greatness of the event in the history of law study, may be observed in the opening paragraph of the lecture. "The general expectation," he said, "of so numerous and respectable an audience, the novelty, and

(I may add) the importance of the duty required from this chair, must unavoidably be productive of great diffidence and apprehensions in him who has the honor to be placed in it. He must be sensible how much will depend upon his conduct in the infancy of a study, which is now first adopted by public academical authority; which has generally been reputed (however unjustly) of a dry and unfruitful nature; and of which the theoretical, elementary parts have hitherto received a very moderate share of cultivation. He cannot but reflect that, if either his plan of instruction be crude and injudicious, or the execution of it lame and superficial, it will cast a damp upon the farther progress of this most useful and most rational branch of learning; and may defeat for a time the public-spirited design of our wise and munificent benefactor."

The lectures were successful to a remarkable degree, and Blackstone was invited to read them privately to the Prince of Wales. This honor he declined, but sent him copies of the lectures for his own perusal and received in return a handsome gratuity. The manuscript notes of the lectures, in four volumes, are now preserved in the library of the Incorporated Law Society of London. Blackstone held the professorship from 1758 to 1766, when he was succeeded by Robert Chambers. In 1761 he married, thus vacating his fellowship of All Souls, but was immediately appointed principal of New Inn Hall, so that he might continue his residence in Oxford and deliver his lectures. Of his lectures as they were being given in December, 1763, we have an unsympathetic account by Jeremy Bentham, who attended them at that time. "I attended with two collegiates of my acquaintance," he writes.[5] "One was Samuel Parker Coke, a descendant of Lord Coke, a gentleman commoner, who afterwards sat in Parliament; the other was Dr. Downes. They both took notes; which I attempted to do, but could not continue it, as my thoughts were occupied in reflecting on what I heard. I immediately detected his fallacy respecting natural rights; I thought his notions very frivolous and illogical about the gravitating downwards of *hæreditas;* and his reasons altogether futile, why it must *descend* and could not *ascend*—an idea, indeed, borrowed from Lord Coke. Blackstone was a formal, precise, and affected lecturer—just what you would expect from the character of his writings: cold, reserved and wary—exhibiting a frigid pride. But his lectures were popular, though the subject did not then excite a widespreading interest, and his attendants were not more than from thirty to fifty." In another place Bentham says:[6] "I, too, heard the lectures; age, sixteen; and even then, no small part of them with rebel ears. The attributes (given by Blackstone to the sovereign), I remember, in particular, stuck in my stomach." Before this time, Blackstone seems to have lost interest in the lectures; for in 1762 an attempt was made to restrain his powers under the will and statutes to perform his duties by deputy, leading him to publish an argument in support of the right. Unquestionably the lectures were now of secondary importance in his affairs; for, in addition to sitting in Parliament as member from Hindon, he was, beginning in 1763, a Bencher of the Middle Temple, Solicitor-General to her Majesty the Queen, and in regular attendance at Westminster Hall. His waning

[5] Works: Bowring ed., 10: 45.
[6] *Ibid.,* 1: 249.

interest in the lectures was due also to the failure of his plan to establish upon the Vinerian foundation a College of the Common Law similar to Trinity Hall, set apart for students of Civil Law, at Cambridge. This plan, though approved by the Delegates of Oxford, was rejected in convocation. He, therefore, resigned his lectureship, which according to Malone[7] had returned him £600 a year.

Blackstone's Commentaries

Before putting behind him altogether the life of the teacher, he had, however, prepared and published the first volume of his Commentaries. This was issued in November, 1765. In the preface he says that, having determined on account of ill health to retire from professorial duties "after the conclusion of the annual course in which he is at present engaged," he was urged by his friends to print "the hints which he had collected for the use of his students." This he was the more willing to do as a matter of protection, since "the notes which were taken by his hearers, have by some of them (too partial in his favor) been thought worth revising and transcribing; and these transcripts have been frequently lent to others. Hence copies have been multiplied, in their nature imperfect if not erroneous; some of which have fallen into mercenary hands, and become the object of clandestine sale. Having therefore so much reason to apprehend a surreptitious impression, he chose rather to submit his own errors to the world, than to seem answerable for those of other men." Clitherow[8] says that a pirated

[7] Prior: Life, p. 431.
[8] 1 Wm. Blackstone's Reports, xvi.

edition was then "either published or preparing for publication in Ireland." No record of this pirated edition has been found, but an unauthorized edition of his Analysis of the Laws of England had been published in Dublin in 1766.

The remaining three volumes of the first edition were issued in 1766, 1768 and 1769 respectively. On the title-page of volume one, Blackstone describes himself as "Vinerian Professor of Law and Solicitor-General to Her Majesty." On the other three volumes he is named merely Solicitor-General. The work is a large quarto printed at the Clarendon Press, of which Blackstone had, in July, 1755, become a Delegate. As an example of bookmaking, with regard to type, paper and style, it is of unusual merit, worthy of the noble destiny of the book itself.

To the writing of the Commentaries there is attached a story which is of some interest. It was current on this side of the Atlantic, for Chancellor Kent wrote the following words on the flyleaf of volume one of his own copy of the first American edition: "Blackstone, it is said, wrote his Commentaries late in the evening, with a bottle of wine before him, and little did he think, as each sentence fell from the glass and pen, of the immense influence it might hereafter exercise upon the laws and usages of his country." The origin of the story has been traced to Sir William Scott, afterwards Lord Stowell, who told it to Dr. Samuel Johnson. It was therefore faithfully recorded by Boswell and in due course printed in his Life of Johnson (Hill edition, 4:91). The conversation took place on Easter Sunday, April 15, 1781. "Dr. Scott of the Commons came in," wrote Boswell. "He talked of its having been said that Addison wrote some of his best pages in The Spectator when warm with wine. Dr. Johnson did not seem willing to admit this. Dr. Scott, as a confirmation of it, related that Blackstone, a sober man, composed his Commentaries with a bottle of port before him; and found his mind invigorated and supported in the fatigue of his great work, by the temperate use of it." When Boswell's account appeared, Scott was concerned at the disclosure and wrote to Blackstone's family to apologize, fearing that from the words used it might be inferred that Blackstone was a drunkard. This we learn from Prior's Life of Edmund Malone (p. 415), where the latter again tells the story. Malone goes on to explain that Blackstone, being of a languid, phlegmatic constitution, needed a cheerful glass of wine to rouse and animate him, and after he returned from college in the evening frequently had some wine left in his room while writing, "in order to correct or prevent the depression sometimes attendant on close study. That he did not use it to excess," he continues, "the Commentaries themselves, one of the most methodical, perspicuous, and elegant books in our language, clearly show." Malone throws further light on Blackstone's character by quoting[9] Sir William Scott to the effect that Blackstone was extremely irritable. He was the only man whom Scott had ever known who acknowledged and lamented his bad temper.

During Blackstone's life, eight complete editions (except that there was no second or third edition of volumes three and four) were issued. There were also pirated issues, published in Dublin, of the fourth and sixth editions. The first American edition was an au-

[9] Prior: Life, p. 431.

thorized reprint of the fourth English edition, published in Philadelphia, with a fifth volume added. Of this edition notice will subsequently be taken. Malone says that the total sum which Blackstone made by his Commentaries, including the profits of his lectures, the sale of the books while he kept the copyright in his own hands, and the final sale of the proprietorship to Mr. Cadell, amounted to fourteen thousand pounds. He estimated that the bookseller in the next twenty years cleared ten thousand pounds. Certainly few law books have run through so many editions and been so generally received with approbation by succeeding generations. By Digby (Preface to Law of Real Property), the Commentaries are said to be "at once the most available and the most trustworthy authority on the law of the eighteenth century." The work not only acquired vogue in England, but was continually cited by continental writers on English law. Even by Bentham it was admitted that Blackstone was the first who, "of all institutional writers, has taught Jurisprudence to speak the language of the scholar and the gentleman." It was this very quality, according to Bentham, which made the doctrines of the Commentaries the more dangerous, since the author is one "whose works have had, beyond comparison, a more extensive circulation, have obtained a greater share of esteem, of applause, and consequently of influence (and that by a title on many grounds indisputable), than any other writer who on that subject has ever yet appeared." [10] To combat their influence, Bentham issued anonymously, in 1776, a "Fragment on Government," in which he attacked the doctrines set forth in the second section of

[10] Works: Bowring ed., 1:227.

Blackstone's Introduction, on the Nature of Laws in General. He printed a second edition, with his name on the title-page, in 1828. The historical preface to this edition sums up the conflict of ideas and of temper between himself and Blackstone; and he does not omit the story that Blackstone, when asked whether he intended to make answer to the Fragment, replied, "No, not even if it had been better written." That Bentham's dislike of all that smacked of Blackstone had not decreased since he listened to his law lectures in 1763 may be seen from the following lurid passages from Bentham's Commonplace Book, written about the year 1785 concerning Blackstone: [11]

"His hand was formed to embellish and corrupt everything it touches. He makes men think they see, in order to prevent their seeing.

"His is the treasure of vulgar errors, where all the vulgar errors that are, are collected and improved.

"He is infected with the foul stench of intolerance, the rankest degree of intolerance that at this day the most depraved organ can endure.

"In him every prejudice has an advocate, and every professional chicanery an accomplice.

"His are crocodile lamentations.

"He carries the disingenuousness of the hireling advocate into the chair of the professor. He is the dupe of every prejudice, and the abettor of every abuse. No sound principles can be expected from that writer whose first object is to defend a system.

"His is the *'fœdum crimen servitutis'*—the foulest of all intellectual blots that can deform a character."

[11] Works: Bowring ed., 10: 141.

A much later criticism is noted by Kent in volume four of his copy of the Commentaries. "Professor Amos," he says, "called Blackstone's Commentaries the charnel house of dead law; but," adds Kent, "it was characteristic of that lecturer to be ever on the reach for pointed sentences." In the same note he quoted Henry J. Stephens, author of a Summary of the Criminal Law, as saying that Blackstone's fourth volume "has become, by the vast alterations in the law, an insufficient and dangerous guide unless accompanied by notes bearing a large proportion in magnitude to the text." Kent's own opinion of volume four is given in his copy of that volume in a note written in 1798. "This fourth volume of Blackstone," he says, "is handsomely written and is rather a light and general analysis of criminal law. It is compiled chiefly from Hawkins and Hale and Barrington and Montesquieu. The two latter have given him much of the ornamental and historical learning. *It requires but ordinary talents and industry to compile such a volume.* Hawkins' Pleas of the Crown is a work of much greater labor and utility. It is indeed a most accurate and profound and perfect disquisition on the English Criminal Law."

President Jefferson did not think the influence of the Commentaries had been good in America; for in discussing the desirability of excluding English legal authorities in the United States, he said in 1813 that one of the consequences would be to "uncanonize Blackstone, whose book, although the most elegant and best digested of our law catalogue, has been perverted more than all others to the degeneracy of legal science. A student finds there a smattering of everything, and his indolence easily persuades him, that if he understands that book, he is master of the whole body of the law." [12] To these criticisms were added in 1815 a general objection to the use of the Commentaries as a means of professional law study. In that year Frederick Ritso, a barrister of Lincoln's Inn, published a book entitled "An Introduction to the Science of the Law" in which he attempted to show the advantages of grounding legal education on Coke's Institutes and Littleton's Tenures, instead of Blackstone's Commentaries. The first seventy-eight pages of his book are devoted to showing that Blackstone is a faulty guide for the lawyer because, in the guise of a professor, he wrote for an audience of laymen and not for law students. He gives many examples "of the sort of loose, inaccurate superficial kind of professional instruction, which is to be picked up from Blackstone's Commentaries," ending with the statement that "in the rank of elementary composition, they might forever have reposed beneath undisturbed laurels; but he who would make them the institute of his professional education, improvidently forces them into an element which is not their own, and lays the foundation for those perilous misunderstandings,—that unlawyer-like jejune smattering,—which informs without enlightening, and leaves its deluded votary at once profoundly ignorant and contented" (p. 77). So great was the criticism from time to time, in which Bentham, Sedgwick and Austin joined, that adherents were quickened in their praise of it; thought and discussion were aroused; and the Commentaries have the distinction of having "created, by repulsion, the later English school of jurisprudence." To Bentham and to all later critics of the faults of omission and commission of Blackstone, perhaps the best answer is the words put

[12] Tucker: Life of Jefferson, 2:327.

into the mouth of Blackstone by Sir Frederick Pollock.[13] "My dear young man," Blackstone is supposed to say, "pray remember that my duty as Vinerian professor was to teach the laws of England, not political philosophy. To be sure, I took over fashionable commonplaces which had nothing to do with the common law, from Burlamaqui and his like. Those were academic ornaments, what you now call frills. I confess I troubled myself little about their coherence with the matters of substance. Then you say I tell you nothing about the practical working of ministerial administration and ignore cabinet government; it is very true. In the common pleas I was judicially aware, as my successors still are, of a Lord Chancellor, secretaries of state, and other great officers; and, moreover, that someone who can at need be impeached or sued must be answerable for everything done in the King's name. We had not your modern statutory departments, with defined statutory powers and duties. Administration was carried on by regular, but extra-legal, methods, behind the screen of legal forms. Is it not largely so to this day? The cabinet was wholly unknown to the law; do your courts know it now? As for the nineteenth century system of party government, it was yet to come. It was not for me to demonstrate to English country gentlemen the working details of their institutions, whose flesh and blood would be before their eyes in Parliament, at assizes and quarter sessions, and so forth, but to show them the legal skeleton. That piece of work, I make bold to say, was not ill done."

[13] Review of H. J. Laski's Political Thought in England from Locke to Bentham. Literary Review, New York Evening Post, November 6, 1920.

The First American Edition

The publication of the first American edition of the Commentaries was an important event in legal annals on this side of the Atlantic. It appeared in 1771–1772 and was the first law book of a general character printed in the Colonies. The first law book printed by them appeared in 1680, "Reasons for the Indictment of the Duke of York," and was followed by a few manuals for the use of local officers,—justices of the peace, sheriffs, magistrates. To one of these manuals, Conductor Generalis, published in New Jersey in 1764,[14] was added a reprint of Blackstone's Treatise on the Law of Descent in Fee Simple, and this was the first of Blackstone's works printed in America. The fame of Blackstone's lectures and Commentaries had, however, spread across the water as early as 1759,[15] and English editions were imported in quantities. Before 1771, 1,000 sets had been shipped to this side. It was this great demand that led to the publication of an American edition. In order to promote success in the undertaking, an appeal to the patriotism of all the Colonies considered as a unit was made. The imprint reads: "America. Printed for the Subscribers by Robert Bell, at the late Union Library, in Third Street, Philadelphia." In the front of volume one is an address

[14] Parker, James: Conductor generalis; or, the office, duty, and authority of justices of the peace. . . . By James Parker, one of his Majesty's justices of the peace for Middlesex County in New Jersey. . . . To which is added, A treatise on the law of descents in fee-simple. By William Blackstone, Esq.; Barrister-at-law, Vinerian professor of the Laws of England . . . Woodbridge in New Jersey: Printed (by James Parker) for, and sold by Garrat Noel, near the Merchant's Coffee-House in New York. MDCCLXIV 8°. xvi., 592 p.

[15] See Warren: American Bar, p. 179.

by the publisher "To the American World" which is worth reproducing in full because of the light which it throws on early American book publishing and the book market.

"The inhabitants of this continent have now an easy and advantageous opportunity of effectually establishing literary manufactures in the British Colonies, at moderate prices calculated for this meridian, the establishment of which will absolutely and eventually produce mental improvement, and commercial expansion, with the additional recommendation of positively saving thousands of pounds to and among the inhabitants of the British Empire in America.—Thus—The importation of one thousand sets of Blackstone's Commentaries, manufactured in Europe, at ten pounds per set, is sending very near ten thousand pounds across the great Atlantic ocean. Whereas—One thousand sets manufactured in America, and sold at the small price of three pounds per set, is an actual saving of seven thousand pounds to the purchasers, and the identical three thousand pounds which is laid out for our own manufactures is still retained in the country being distributed among manufacturers and traders, whose residence upon the continent of course causeth the money to circulate from neighbor to neighbor, and by this circulation in America there is a great probability of its revolving to the very hands from which it originally migrated.—

"American Gentlemen or Ladies who, at this juncture, retain any degree of that antient and noble, but now almost extinguished, affection denominated patriotism, and are now pleased to exemplify it by extending with celerity and alacrity their auspicious patronage through the cheap mode of reposing their names and residences (no money expected till the delivery of an equivalent) with any Bookseller or Printer on the continent, as intentional purchasers of any of the literary works now in contemplation to be reprinted by subscription in America —will render an essential service to the community, by encouraging native manufactures—and therefore deserve to be had in grateful remembrance—by their country—by posterity—and by their much obliged, humble servant, the Publisher—

"Robert Bell.

"Memorandum. This Volume can only be sold to those GENTLEMEN who are willing to subscribe for the whole of those celebrated COMMENTARIES, by giving in their Names as ENCOURAGERS.

" **All Independent Gentlemen and Scholars, as well as every Magistrate, civil Officer and Lawyer, ought to possess this SPLENDID and USEFUL WORK: Therefore the EDITOR hopeth, Patriotism to encourage native FABRICATIONS; with the Advantage of saving seven Pounds in the Purchase of ten pounds Worth.—The British Edition being sold at Ten Pounds Pennsylvania Currency, together with that innate Thirst for Knowledge, which is so admirably ingrafted in the Contexture of the human Mind;—will nobly animate all, whose Ideas are expanded in search of Knowledge, to encourage this AMERICAN Edition.

" 'Content of Spirit must from Science flow,
For 'tis a Godlike Attribute to know.'
"PRIOR."

In volume four are printed the names of the subscribers. The list is headed by the British Governors of Virginia, New Jersey, Bahama Islands, Bermuda, Pennsylvania, Connecticut and East Florida; and includes the names of John Adams, George Clinton, Nathaniel Green, John Jay, Sir William Johnson, Gouverneur Morris, Robert Morris, Isaac Roosevelt, St. George Tucker, Oliver Walcott and James Wilson. There are 800 names in the list, and besides the attorneys, judges and office-holders, are included (as shown by the description after many of the names) cabinetmakers, farmers, merchants, students, printers, booksellers, bookbinders, steel manufacturers, tavern keepers, naval officers, scriveners and professors. The booksellers of Boston subscribed for 239 copies; those of Charleston for 89, of Philadelphia for 84, of New York for 60, of Norfolk, Williamsburgh and Winchester, Virginia, for 97.[16] In all, 1,400 sets were ordered in advance. In his copy, Kent notes that "the price was $8 and the mechanical execution is creditable to the press of the period." So notable was the demand for the book in America that Edmund Burke in his great conciliation speech in the House of Commons, March 22, 1776, said: "I have been told by an eminent bookseller, that in no branch of his business, after tracts of popular devotion, were so many books as those of the law exported to the plantations. The colonists have now fallen into the way of printing them for their own use. I hear that they have sold nearly as many of Blackstone's Commentaries in America as in England."

That the publishers worked under difficulties appears at several places in the edition. At the foot of page 27, volume one, where a Greek quotation appeared in the English edition, the editor appends the following note:

[16] Warren: History of American Bar, p. 178.

"There being no Greek characters at present in Philadelphia, we hope the learned reader will accept the Greek in Roman letters." At the end of the table of contents is the following: "If any reader of this edition meets with some words uncommonly spelled, he is requested, not hastily to blame the *American* editor; because report sayeth, the last British edition was corrected under the immediate inspection of the learned author, and it has of late been the practice of several great men to spell many words in their own peculiar manner.—Therefore, the *American* editor, to make this American edition a perfect transcript of the last British edition, hath adhered to it as literally as possible."

After 1766, as has been said, Blackstone had no active connection with Oxford University, and devoted himself to legal practice, the preparation of his Commentaries, and his duties to the successive public offices to which he was appointed. In 1768 he was returned as a member of Parliament from Westbury, but sat only two years. In this Parliament an incident happened which has to do with the Commentaries. John Wilkes, member elected from Middlesex, was expelled from the House on February 3, 1769, "for having printed and published a seditious libel, and three obscene and impious libels." Being a popular hero, Wilkes was re-elected three successive times during the same Parliament, and as often refused a seat by the Commons. There was acrimonious debate on the question whether a member expelled by the House was or was not eligible for re-election in the same Parliament, and Blackstone, then also Solicitor-General to the Queen, took sides against Wilkes. At the close of his speech he was confronted by Mr. Grenville with a passage from the first volume of his Commentaries (1st ed. 1:169) where the grounds for disqualification were enumerated, and where no such case as Wilkes' was given. There was a perceptible pause in the debate for Blackstone to reply, but he was not prepared to do so. The controversy was not ended by the seating of Luttrell as member, and the house and the electors were sharply divided on the legality of the election. Then began a war of pamphleteers in which Samuel Johnson, Sir Philip Francis (Philo Junius), Sir William Meredith and Blackstone participated. Meredith's first pamphlet was entitled "The Question Stated." Blackstone replied in a letter dated June 28, 1769. In it he successfully defended himself from the alleged inconsistency between "the thoughts of the professor," and "the words of the politician." He had in his Commentaries, he said, "recounted only such disabilities as had then [in 1765] been adjudged or created; and among these, such only as are permanent, general, and applicable to whole classes of men." Nevertheless, in the next edition of volume one, published in 1770 (1 : 176), he took pains to include in the list of disqualifications for election a phrase which would cover Wilkes' case. This subjected him to further ridicule, so that a favorite toast at Opposition banquets became, "The *first* edition of Dr. Blackstone's Commentaries on the Laws of England."

Blackstone's Reports

In spite of the enemies created by Parliamentary strife, and the violent opposition shown to his Commentaries, Blackstone's reputation was now at its height. His position of learning was, in 1770, recognized by the appointment to be judge of the Common Pleas. For a few months he was transferred to the King's Bench, but then served in the Common Pleas until his death on February 14, 1780. Of this appointment, an astigmatic view is given by Bentham.[17] "Lord Shelburne had been the making of Blackstone," he wrote. "The Lord had been in personal favor with George III. He introduced the lecturer, and made the monarch sit to be lectured: so he himself told me. The lecturer, as anybody may see, shewed the King how Majesty is God upon earth: Majesty could do no less than make him a judge for it." As a judge, Blackstone was exceedingly cautious and conservative. His most famous decision was in the case of Perrin v. Blake, in which he discussed the rule in Shelley's case.

After his death, it was found that his will contained a clause directing "that his manuscript Reports of Cases determined in Westminster Hall, taken by himself, and contained in several large notebooks be published after his decease; and that the produce thereof be carried to, and considered as part of his personal estate." There were five of these notebooks, all written by his own hand, and prepared for the press, with index and tables. They begin with 1746 when he was called to the Bar and extend through Michaelmas Term, 1779. The reports, first published in two volumes, under the editorship of his brother-in-law, James Clitherow, in 1780 (London), were reprinted in 1781, and in Dublin, 1789. The second edition, revised and corrected, was published in 1828. Many of the reported cases are in fragmentary form, which leads some writers, in spite of Clitherow's statement that they were prepared for press by the author, to believe that Blackstone intended to give them further revision.

[17] Works: Bowring ed. 1:249.

For many years they were not considered the best authority,[18] but after the publication of the second edition, they began to be cited with favor.

[18] See 1 Johnson's Cases, 45; 1 Douglas 93 note.

CHAPTER VI

James Kent and His Commentaries

The story of James Kent, Chief Justice of the New York Supreme Court, Chancellor of the Court of Chancery, first Professor of Law at Columbia College, author of Commentaries on American Law, is a chronicle of everyday life, which charms because of its simplicity, the logic of its development, and the strength of character which it unfolds. His was a life of cleanliness, domestic happiness, devotion to duty, industry, rigid self-discipline, intellectual vigor and capacity for friendship. But virtue was not with him its only reward. From poverty he rose to comparative wealth, from professional obscurity he rose to pre-eminence, and he left behind him, besides a long line of judicial decisions, a classical treatise which is to American jurisprudence what Blackstone is to England's. He lived to reap the reward of labor, and before he died at the age of eighty-five, there were present all evidences necessary to prove that he had made for himself an honored place in history.

With no attempt to find in the story striking episodes, heroic achievements, crises met, disasters borne with fortitude, nor even to point a moral for the law student of to-day, the tale is here recounted of those events which led up to the preparation and publication of his Commentaries. The story will be told largely in Kent's own words or in the words of his contemporaries. This is possible because of several fortunate circumstances. Although Kent wrote no formal autobiography, he did pre-

James Kent

pare in 1828 at the request of Thomas Washington of Nashville, Tennessee, a connected account of his life to that time;[1] and at his death extensive obituaries were prepared.[2] He left fifteen manuscript volumes of diaries covering the period from 1797 to 1846, with special reference to thirty-one journeys which he took; he was an inveterate writer of letters many of which have been printed in the correspondence of men of his time, and he preserved the replies which he received. The diaries and other papers of Kent have been deposited in the Manuscripts Division of the Library of Congress. Of the papers, there are eleven bound volumes in addition to the diaries. Before these manuscripts were given to the National Library, William Kent, great-grandson of James Kent, prepared a volume of Memoirs and Letters, which was published in 1898, and consists largely of excerpts from Kent's own writings. Through this publication, access is given to the essential contents of many of the original manuscripts. Moreover, a portion of Kent's law library is the prized possession of the Columbia University Law Library. It consists of 749 volumes presented to the University in 1911 by Mr. Edwin C. Kent. It can be only a part of the original collection, for Kent made continual additions to his library by purchase, and in his later years was the recipient of gifts of books from many prominent legal writers. Writing in 1828, Kent said: "My library, which started from nothing, grew with my growth, and it has now attained upwards of 3,000 volumes; and it is pretty well selected,

[1] Southern Law Review, 1: 381–391; Virginia Law Register, 3: 563–571.

[2] Obituary of Kent, Humphrey's Tennessee Reports, 27: ix–xix.; Duer, Discourse on the Life of Kent. New York, 1848.

for there is scarcely a work, authority or document, referred to in the three volumes of my Commentaries, but what has a place in my own library. Next to my wife, my library has been the source of my greatest pleasure and devoted attachment."[3] The association of these volumes with the first professor of law of Columbia University and with America's foremost legal classic gives them special value to the Columbia Law School; but for another reason they are a priceless possession. They are filled with annotations in his own hand,—not only of remarks, criticisms and observations on the contents of the books, on the authors of them, and personages and events mentioned in them,—but notes of intimate affairs of his own professional and family life. It has been truly said of him that he studied pen in hand. Inserted in the volumes are also letters received by him from eminent men of his day, in many of which are references to events of his professional life, and testimonials of the esteem in which he and his work were held by his contemporaries. From these sources the writer has compiled the following account, using the words of others whenever the progress of the narrative would permit.

Kent was born in Fredericksburgh precinct, Dutchess County, New York, on July 31, 1763, less than a year before Edward Livingston was born. His father was a lawyer, and his grandfather, Reverend Elisha Kent, a Presbyterian minister. He came of good stock,—substantial people, fairly well-to-do, and possessed of education and refinement. Like his grandfather, Elisha Kent, he graduated from Yale College (1777–1781); but his course of study was several times interrupted by the

[3] Southern Law Review, 1: 385.

events of the Revolutionary War. During one of these periods he made the decision as to the career which he was to follow. In one of the Memoranda which he left he says: "When the college was broken up and dispersed in July, 1779, by the British, I retired to a country village, and, finding Blackstone's Commentaries, I read the four volumes. Parts of the work struck my taste, and the work inspired me, at the age of fifteen, with awe, and I fondly determined to be a lawyer."

After his graduation, his father found a place for him in the law offices of Attorney-General Egbert Benson at Poughkeepsie (November, 1781), where he remained until admitted to the New York Supreme Court Bar in January, 1785. He has told with much detail what was the method of his study and what books he read. Among these were Grotius, Puffendorf, Smollett's History of England, Rapin's English History, Hale's History of the Common Law and Blackstone again. Most of these he abridged, making copious extracts. This labor required much determination, for he lacked the inspiration and guidance of a teacher; and moreover he found the study of law difficult. Writing in 1782, to Simeon Baldwin, a classmate at Yale, he said: "Law, I must frankly confess, is a field which is uninteresting and boundless. Notwithstanding, it leads forward to the first stations in the State. The study is so encumbered with voluminous rubbish and the baggage of folios that it requires uncommon assiduity and patience to manage so unwieldy a work. Yet this adage often serves to steel my courage and smooth the rugged moments of despair: 'The harder the conflict the more glorious the triumph.' "[4]

[4] Memoirs, ed. by Wm. Kent, p. 16.

On being admitted to the Bar, he found himself without funds and in debt to the amount of four hundred dollars; yet four months later he was married to Elizabeth Bailey, daughter of Colonel John Bailey, of Poughkeepsie. He was twenty-one and his bride sixteen years of age. He had no money except what he might earn, and his house was small and scantily furnished; yet, as he afterwards said, they "lived neat and simple and snug." In the same month (April, 1785) he entered into a law partnership with Gilbert Livingston. He was not overpressed with business, and soon began to devote himself to study of the classics, the impetus coming from the following incident, afterwards related by him. "At the June circuit, 1786," he says, "I saw Edward Livingston (afterwards the codifier for Louisiana), and he had a pocket Horace and read some passages to me, and pointed out their beauties, assuming that I well understood Horace. I said nothing, but was stung with shame and mortification. I purchased immediately Horace and Virgil, a dictionary and grammar, and a Greek lexicon and grammar, and the Testament, and formed my resolution, promptly and decidedly, to recover the lost languages." (Memoirs, p. 24.) This was the beginning of a lifelong devotion to classical literature. That the incident was firmly fixed in his mind is shown by further reference to it quoted at the close of Chapter VII. The next seven years of his life were of consequence in his career because of his devotion to study, and on account of the friendships that he made. He came in close touch with the political leaders of the state when, in 1788, the New York Convention convened at Poughkeepsie to consider ratification of the Constitution of the United States. It was then that he first became acquainted with Alexander Hamilton, his senior by only seven years, but already a national figure. Throughout his life, Kent was a pronounced Federalist, and his connections were such that he was twice elected to the New York Assembly, which then met in New York City. He supported John Jay in the contested Gubernatorial election which had been awarded to Clinton, and thus roused against himself the political adherents of the latter, among whom was his brother-in-law, Theodorus Bailey. In 1793, he ran for Congress, but was defeated by Bailey. This check to his political career can, in retrospect, be seen to have been fortunate. It was the incentive for leaving Poughkeepsie, giving up his legal partnership, and devoting himself to judicial preferment. In April, 1793, with his wife and daughter, he moved to New York City. "I carried with me," he says, "a small, well-chosen library, scanty furniture, and £100 in cash; leaving real property behind to the value of £200; and this was the total result of my eight years' settlement at Poughkeepsie. But I owed nothing and came to the city with good character and with a scholar's reputation." He did not, however, immediately prosper. Little business came his way, his daughter and his father, who came to live with him, became ill, and he lived in a "narrow, dirty street." To meet his necessities he was obliged to call on his brother, Moss Kent, for financial assistance.

It was at this point that both his scholarly attainments and his capacity for making friends came to his rescue. "While at Poughkeepsie," he says, "my Federal celebrity procured my acquaintance and friendship with several distinguished men in New York, such as Chief Justice Jay, Judge Hobart of the Supreme Court, and Colonel Troup and Edward Livingston. It was the character I had insensibly acquired as a scholar and a Federalist and a presumed (though it was not true) well-read lawyer that the very first year that I removed to New York, I was appointed a Professor of Law in Columbia College. The influence of Dr. S. Bard, of Judge Hobart, of B. Livingston, Edward Livingston, and probably of Chief Justice Jay, procured me the appointment." This timely appointment was made on December 24, 1793, but he did not begin his lectures until November 17, 1794. During the intervening period, he devoted himself to preparing his lectures and studying in the originals the works of Bynkershoeck, Quintilian and Cicero, and the English reports and digests. From November 17, 1794, to February 27, 1795, he delivered twenty-six lectures, two a week, to "seven students and thirty-six gentlemen, chiefly lawyers and law students who did not belong to the college." In another place he describes this group as being made up of "gentlemen of the first rank in the city." The audience which he addressed was similar in character to that to which Blackstone's first lectures at Oxford had been given. Writing on March 1, 1795, to his brother, Moss Kent, he says: "On Friday last, I closed my lectures at college and I feel now restored to my ancient freedom. Twenty-six lectures have been delivered, extending not only through the Constitution and Jurisprudence of the Union, the Constitution of this and the other States, but our doctrine of real property. My first plan was to examine the law of personal property, including the commercial branches, and the system of our criminal code. But I found myself absolutely unable to complete the whole, and was obliged to leave this first course imperfect. . . . I am satisfied that my lectures have been well received, and that my expectations are answered"

(Memoirs, p. 74). He held a different opinion of these lectures when, in an autobiographical sketch dated October 6, 1828, he wrote: "I have long since discovered them to have been slight and trashy productions. I wanted judicial labors to teach me precision."

Kent's first law lecture was published in 1794 at the request of the College Trustees, with the following title, "An introductory lecture to a course of law lectures, delivered November 17, 1794." (New York, Printed by Francis Childs, 1794. 12°. 23p.) It is a general sketch of the course of lectures which he was about to give, and it closes with a statement of the particular reasons why the study of the law seemed to him to be appropriate at that time. These closing words are so apposite to our own time that they might have been written in the year 1921: "The events which are rapidly crowding the present era," he says, "are to be deemed among the most solemn, and the most important in their consequences of any which have hitherto been displayed in the history of mankind. Great revolutions are taking place in the European world, in government, in policy and in morals, and a new turn will be given to the habits of thinking, and probably to the destination of human society. A total demolition of the ancient fabrics, and the most daring hand of innovation, may possibly be expedient in the eastern continent, to recall society to its original principles of simplicity and freedom; and to dissolve the long, intricate, and oppressive chain of subordination, which has degraded the principal nations of Europe. . . . But . . . we in this country ought to be extremely careful, not to pass along unconscious of the labors of the Patriots who effected our Revolution; nor let the admirable fabrics of our Constitutions and the all-pervading freedom of our common law, be left unheeded or despised."

The publication of this lecture gave to Kent a wider celebrity than would have been otherwise possible. That it was studied and criticised with care is shown by three letters written by John Adams to his son Charles, February 14–15, 1795 (Memoirs, pp. 64–73). This notice alone was no small distinction for a struggling young lawyer of thirty-one; and at the time, as we have seen, Kent felt that he had acquitted himself with credit. He was, however, doomed to disappointment, for when he began his second course of lectures in November, 1795, only two students put in an appearance. To these he read thirty-one lectures in his law office, eking out an audience by the addition of his clerks. Thinking that further publicity might bring him more students, he then published at his own expense, his "three preliminary lectures, together with a summary of the entire course." This pamphlet was entitled "Dissertations; being the preliminary part of a course of law lectures." (New York, Printed by George Forman, for the author, 1795.) His third course was announced in the newspapers, but no students at all applied for it. He thereupon, on May 2, 1797, sent in his letter of resignation to the College. It was not, however, accepted, and on the very next day the institution conferred on him the degree of Doctor of Laws. "In the winter of 1797 and 1798, in my office," the record concludes, "I read lectures to six or eight students, and in April, 1798, I finally resigned the office." Thus came to an end the first law lectures given in Columbia University, and the first law professorship of the institution, the period of which extended from December 24, 1793, to April, 1798.

Kent now turned his attention to other fields. In February, 1796, he was appointed Master in Chancery by Governor Jay. There being only one other Master in New York City, this office was lucrative. In May of the same year, he was elected to the New York Assembly, and in March, 1797, he was appointed Recorder of the City of New York, retaining at the same time the Mastership. The Recordership was the first judicial office held by Kent, and for that reason was much to his liking. The income from his two offices was large, and he was thus able in a few years to acquire property which relieved him of all financial worries, and enabled him to indulge his desire for classical and legal literature. "I keep making daily additions to my library," he wrote in July, 1796, "which I regard as the repository of my happiest pursuits." But new duties were soon to be his. On February 6, 1798, he was appointed Judge of the New York Supreme Court. Thus, by three successive appointments, he was amply rewarded by Governor Jay for championing his cause in the contested election with Clinton; a reward, however, which was not misplaced upon one who had well equipped himself for high office. By accepting the judgeship Kent gave up his more lucrative offices and definitely determined upon a judicial career. Thus honorably placed at the age of thirty-five, he took up his home once more in Poughkeepsie, which he had left only a few years before in such unhappy circumstances. "I removed to Poughkeepsie," he writes, "and found myself upon my ancient ground after an absence of five years. But so great and so rapid a change in so short a space of time few persons have met with. I went to New York poor, without patronage, and had a most gloomy and distressing introduction to the city life. In five years I had run through several honorable offices and attained one of the highest respect in the community. I had collected not only a large and valuable library, and a neat and valuable stock of furniture, but I returned say at least £1,000 richer than when I went." He remained in Poughkeepsie only one year, moving to Albany in 1799 where he continued to live for twenty-four years. In 1804 he was appointed Chief Justice of the Supreme Court. In the same year (December, 1804), William Johnson was appointed Supreme Court Reporter, thus bringing into professional relationship two men already friends, a connection that continued until Kent retired from the bench twenty years afterward. So close was the friendship and so great the esteem of the judge for the Reporter, that the former subsequently dedicated his Commentaries to Johnson in the following words: "You have reported every opinion which I gave in term time, and thought worth reporting, during the five and twenty years that I was a judge at law and in equity, with the exception of the short intervals occupied by Mr. Caines' Reports. During that long period, I had the happiness to maintain a free, cordial, and instructive intercourse with you; and I feel unwilling now to close my labors as an author, and withdraw myself finally from the public eye, without leaving some memorial of my grateful sense of the value of your friendship, and my reverence for your character."

Kent's decisions as Supreme Court Justice were notable, as may be seen by an examination of the volumes of Johnson's Cases, 1799 to 1803, and his Reports, 1806 to 1814. For the development of American jurisprudence the year 1804 was of great importance, for in that year the New York Legislature passed an act creating the office of official reporter, Kent was appointed Chief Justice, and Johnson, Supreme Court Reporter. Kent had already instituted the practice of written opinions, and now with an official whose duty it was to record them, there was laid the second "stone in the subsequently erected temple of our jurisprudence." "I gradually acquired preponderating influence with my brethren," says Kent, "and the volumes in Johnson, after I became Chief Justice in 1804, show it. The first practice was for each judge to give his portion of opinions, when we all agreed, but that gradually fell off, and, for the last two or three years before I left the Bench, I gave most of them. I remember that in eighth Johnson all the opinions for one term are '*per curiam*.' The fact is I wrote them all and proposed that course to avoid exciting jealousy, and many a *per curiam* opinion was so inserted for that reason."

The year 1804 witnessed also an event which was a source of great sorrow to Kent, the death by the hand of Burr of Alexander Hamilton. The grief must have been the greater because Kent was indirectly connected with the quarrel which was the occasion for the duel. There had been personal feeling between Hamilton and Burr, which was brought to a head when the latter demanded an explanation of a statement in a letter signed by Charles D. Cooper, which said that "General Hamilton and Judge Kent have declared, in substance, that they looked upon Mr. Burr to be a dangerous man, and one who ought not to be trusted with the reins of government." In the Memoirs, edited by William Kent, it is remarked with surprise that among Kent's notes the only reference to the duel is the following, written in a volume of newspapers giving accounts of the events of the controversy and duel: "General Hamilton killed in a duel with Col. Burr." To this brief reference we can now add the following, written by Kent on a manuscript volume entitled "Case of Harry Croswell v. The People," which is deposited in the New York Public Library: "*Mem.* General Hamilton died at N. York on Thursday, July 12th, 1804, of a wound he received in a duel fought with Col. Burr the morning of the preceding day. He was the pride and glory of our country, and his memory was honored with the deepest expressions of the public veneration and sorrow. He was of the age of forty-eight or thereabouts."

On February 24, 1814, Kent was appointed Chancellor of the New York Court of Chancery. This court had not hitherto been of great influence, although it had existed since 1701 when its erection by the British Governor and Council had rendered it unpopular. Kent therefore was loth to accept the appointment; yet it opened up to him the greatest opportunity of his judicial career. "I took the court," he says, "as if it had been a new institution, and never before known in the United States. I had nothing to guide me, and was left at liberty to assume all such English Chancery powers and jurisdiction as I thought applicable under our Constitution. This gave me grand scope, and I was checked only by the revision of the Senate, or Court of Errors." Before Kent's time, the decisions of the court had not been published, but in accordance with an act of April 13, 1814, it was made the duty of the State Reporter to publish such decisions as the Chancellor should deem important. Johnson, therefore, while continuing his Supreme Court Reports, began a new series, Johnson's Chancery Reports, which had run to seven volumes when both he and Kent went out of office. Kent was practically the creator of equity jurisdiction in the United States, and the joint work of Johnson and Kent, the latter the creator, the former the recorder, was fittingly closed by the dedication of the last volume of Chancery Reports to Kent. The words of dedication are fulsome, and might be attributed to friendship and gratitude, but they have been concurred in by every subsequent student of American equity jurisprudence.

Kent retired from the Bench at the age of sixty, on July 31, 1823. "Compelled, by the policy of the Constitution," reads Johnson's dedication, "to retire, at the full meridian of your faculties and fame, from that high station which you have so long filled with honor, the splendor that surrounds your character will diffuse its beams over the remainder of your life." In spite of the high station that he had attained, and the numerous expressions of public esteem that came to him, Chancellor Kent retired with feelings of annoyance and sadness. He felt aggrieved that some of his recent decisions as Chancellor had been overruled by the Court of Errors,—it was hinted with a political motive,—and he was obliged to lay down his work not because incapacitated by years, but because he had reached the retirement age of sixty, fixed by the Constitution. Being in perfect health, and accustomed for many years to exacting judicial labors, it was necessary that he find some new task, not only to occupy his mind, but to supplement his income. He had no inclination to return to the active practice of law. "I would rather saw wood," was his reaction. His friends, knowing that retirement was unavoidable, sought to find place for him where his unimpaired powers could be used. Daniel Webster in 1822 proposed that Kent be offered the Presidency of Dartmouth College, and in

1823 he expressed the hope in a letter to Joseph Story that Kent might be appointed to the United States Supreme Court. Others sought to have him serve on the Committee of Revision of the New York laws. James I. Roosevelt suggested that he prepare a work on equity jurisprudence.[5] However, none of these possibilities came to pass. He took up his residence in New York City, where lived his eldest daughter, and devoted himself to giving opinions in the capacity of "chamber counsel." Almost immediately he was offered his former post of Professor of Law at Columbia College, which had not been occupied since his retirement from it in 1798. Writing on October 6, 1828, he says: "It had no salary, but I must do something for a living, and I undertook (but exceedingly against my inclination) to write and deliver law lectures. In the two characters of chamber counsel and college lecturer, I succeeded by steady perseverance, beyond my most sanguine expectations, and upon the whole, the five years I have lived here in this city since 1823, have been happy and prosperous." [6]

Of his lectures at this time, and of two of his students, we learn through his own memoranda written on the fly-leaves of his own copy of the first edition of volume one of his Commentaries, now preserved in the Columbia University Law Library. "*Mem.* I removed from Albany to the City of New York October 29, 1823, & about the same time I was appointed Professor of Law in Columbia College.

"My *Introductory Lecture* was delivered in the College Hall February 2d, 1824, & was published by the Trustees of the College.

[5] Butler: Revision and the revisers, p. 7.
[6] Southern Law Review, 1:390.

"*My first Course* consisted of 30 Lectures, & they were delivered between the 6th of Feby. & 18th May both inclusive, on Tuesdays & Fridays. 33 Gentlemen attended this first Course & 14 private students also attended & underwent a private Examination every Saturday on the two preceding Lectures of the week.

"*My second Course* consisted of 50 Lectures, delivered in College Hall between the 8th November 1824 & April 13, 1825 & 21 gentlemen attended my public Lectures & 15 students also attended them & two private Lectures in each week on the College Lectures. I also continued the course of private Lectures on the Practice of the Courts (& they were chiefly *ore tenus*) between the 13' of April and the 27th of April when I terminated my second Course. During the early part of this second Course I instituted a moot or debating club for my private students and they met every Saturday, and discussed in written or set speeches the theme and according to the arrangement assigned the preceding week.

"*My third Course* of law Lectures was confined entirely to my private office. It commenced the 4th Monday in October 1825 & was delivered daily for five days in a week & from 9 to 10 A. M. between that time & the 22d April 1826. This class consisted of 13 students.

"*Mem. George W. Baker* of Elizabeth Town in New Jersey, attended faithfully my 2d & 3d course of Lectures as a private student. He also was a regular clerk to my Son & was a modest, intelligent, fine & lovely youth. He was obliged to leave the office in the Autumn of 1826 on account of ill health, & he died at his father's House April 10'–1827, & would have been 21 years of age had he lived until May of that year. I attended his Funeral April 11th from his Father's House 3 miles below Elizabeth Town N. J.—

"—*Edward Tacknor Lowell* of Boston attended my two first Courses of Lectures. He was educated at Harvard College. He spent (after he left me) two years study & travel in Europe. While in France he took an Instructor in the Civil & French law. He attended the Courts & Parliament in England. He died in Boston of the consumption in 1828 at the age of 25, & was just prepared to take a distinguished station at the Bar."

Kent did not enjoy the preparation of lectures nor the delivery of them. "They give me a good deal of trouble and anxiety," he wrote on November 9, 1824. "I am compelled to study and write all the time, as if I was under the whip and spur." And later, "having got heartily tired of lecturing I abandoned it." His second essay as a teacher, therefore, was made with no great enthusiasm and was ended with relief; but it was the occasion for the most enduring achievement of his life. The idea of publishing his lectures was first suggested to him by his son, William Kent. He had no idea of publishing them when he delivered them. So, at the age of sixty-three he set about rewriting the lectures, and published them in 1826 as volume one of his Commentaries. The book was published at his own expense, the cost in sheets being $1,076.27. I find no record of the number of copies printed, but the number was sufficient to last until 1829. This fact is noted in his copy, above referred to, as follows:

"*Mem.* In January & Feby. 1829, I found the 1′ Vol. had run out, owing to the extra call for it at West Point & elsewhere, & I employed G. F. Hopkins to reprint the 1′ Vol. page for page—total cost of 500 Volumes of it $550—I made some additions to the Notes, & corrected all the little mistakes I had discovered in that 1′ Edit.—I did not call the *reprint of the 1′ Vol.* a 2d Edit.—I only meant it for to supply the *Extra Call* for the 1′ Volume, and it resembles this first Volume as nearly as need be, though I deem it more correct & perfect."

Although enthusiasm for teaching had been lacking, the writing out of his lectures with a view to publication was of genuine interest, enhancing the value of the association that he had had, so he writes in his preface, with "a collection of interesting young gentlemen of fine talents and pure character, who placed themselves under my instruction, and in whose future welfare a deep interest is felt." It was his original intention to complete the work in two volumes (Preface to first volume), but when embarked on the task of writing the second volume he found that he needed more space. In revising his lectures he found that "some parts required to be suppressed, others to be considerably enlarged, and the arrangement of the whole to be altered and improved." His preface announces therefore that a third volume will be necessary. This preface is dated November 17, 1827. But this plan was again changed while he was at work on the third volume, for in September, 1828, he wrote to his brother: "I am printing a third volume of Commentaries and correcting a proof of eight pages daily. I have near two hundred pages already printed, and I shall be obliged to print a fourth volume. I cannot crowd what I have into the third volume, including a large index." This determination was confirmed in the preface to the third volume, dated October 10, 1828, where he announced a fourth volume to be devoted to the "doctrine of real estates."

By November, he was ready to start on the new volume, but it was written with difficulty, a fact which may give encouragement to the modern student of real property. On January 2, 1830, he wrote: "I am busy, very busy with my fourth volume, but the subjects are very abstruse and perplexing, and I move very slowly and warily through the mazes of contingent remainders, executory devises, uses, trusts, and powers, and the modifications which they have received by our Revised Statutes." The volume was however finished during the year. In lieu of a preface, he placed in this volume a dedication of the whole set to his old friend William Johnson.

The reception of the successive volumes was such that, by December 22, 1830, every complete set of the Commentaries had been disposed of by Kent. He seems to have handled the sale himself, and, as has already been noted, the work was published at his own expense. On the above date he wrote to his brother: "I have just completed the sale of all the entire sets of my Commentaries, though I have a good many odd volumes of the first, third, and fourth volumes. The first is separately wanted for academies, and the third and fourth to supply defective sets in the hands of former purchasers. I shall probably, before the end of next year, prepare myself for printing a new and corrected, and somewhat enlarged edition. This I shall not do until the booksellers have had sufficient opportunity to sell what is on hand, nor do I declare any such intentions." The second edition was ready for the printers in August, 1832, and came from the press in the same year. The "Advertisement" to this edition is dated April 23, 1832. The third edition was finished in April, 1836, and published in the same year. In Kent's personal copy of volume one of this edition is inserted a letter (dated August 10, 1836) from Judge S. S. Wilde of the Massachusetts Supreme Court. Written on this letter in Kent's hand is the following note, giving interesting information concerning the price and the sale arrangements for this edition.

"*Mem.* The 3d Edit. of the Commentaries bound in sheep are sold at retail by Little & Co. (Boston) at $12.60, and they are sold to them and others in large quantities in sheets folded at $9 on a twelve months' credit—April, 1838."

Two other editions appeared in the author's lifetime, the fourth in 1840, and the fifth in 1844. A sixth edition was published in 1848, the year after his death; but it was prepared for publication by him, for on March 22, 1847, he wrote to his son William: "I have got quite startled about the decreasing number of my Commentaries. In reckoning up the number of sets left, I find that I have but 499 sets out of the original number of 3,000 left, and of that 499 there are 150 less of Vol. 1, so that, in fact, I have left unsold but 349 entire sets. I must begin a new edition next autumn. I hope I shall have strength, health, and resolution enough to go through with it without calling on you." This edition bears the imprint of the son, William Kent, and the Advertisement, dated January 17, 1848, announces that "the printing of the sixth edition of Kent's Commentaries was commenced in October, 1847, during the life of the author. His death, on the 12th of December, in the same year, devolved upon another the task of supervising the edition, and correcting the press." This was therefore the last edition prepared by Chancellor Kent, the seventh edition, which appeared in 1851, being edited by William Kent and Dorman B. Eaton. Up to the present there have been fourteen editions, the last appearing in 1896; and many eminent men have served as editors, including Justice Oliver W. Holmes. Part I. of volume 1, on International Law, has twice been separately printed, in 1866 and in 1878, under the editorship of John T. Abdy. Part II. of the same volume, on the Constitution of the United States, was translated into German and published in Heidelberg in 1836; and into Spanish and published in Mexico City in 1878. The portion relating to commercial and maritime law was separately published in Edinburgh in 1837.

Of the reputation, standing and permanent value of the work, there are many evidences besides the constant demand for new editions. Many letters were received by the Chancellor from eminent lawyers of his day, commending the work, and many of these are preserved in the Columbia University Law Library inserted in the volumes of the Kent collection. On the publication of the fourth volume of the first edition, Chief Justice Savage wrote (May 6, 1830): "Your Commentaries will remain a living testimonial of your learning and industry to future generations. Your labors have contributed more than those of any other individual to elevate the American judicial character." Andrew Amos of the London University said (May 12, 1831): "I have represented them [the Commentaries] to the law class of the London University as containing a general view of the principles of English not less than of American jurisprudence the most learned and enlightened and at the same time the most candid and unprejudiced that I can put into their hands." Thomas Wharton, Pennsylvania Supreme Court Reporter, wrote him on August 25th, 1836: "I have always thought and said that your Commentaries are superior to those of Sir. Wm. Blackstone as a whole—looking at the depth and accuracy of the learning of the English law and the breadth and beauty of the illustrations from foreign jurisprudence." On receiving a copy of the third edition, Judge Samuel Putnam of Massachusetts wrote: "The generations to come will gratefully speak your name, and of your learning and devotion to truth and justice: and the influence of your virtues and talents will be felt by civilized man wherever he may be found, in all time to come." "Your work," wrote Judge Joseph Story, August 13, 1836, "must forever remain the true standard for all future American text-writers." On January 1st, 1837, Charles Sumner wrote: "When I think of the good you have done, in promoting the study of jurisprudence, by the publication of your Commentaries . . . I cannot but envy you the feelings which you must enjoy. The mighty tribute of gratitude is silently offered to you from every student of the law in our whole country. There is not one, who has found his toilsome way cheered and lighted by the companionship of your labors, who would not speak as I now do, if he had the privilege of addressing you." And again on April 5, 1836, Sumner wrote: "Your admirable Commentaries . . . have now become the manual of the practitioner, as they have since their first publication been the Institute of the student." On March 11, 1837, Chief Justice Mellen of Maine wrote: "I consider those volumes as constituting a Law Bible, in respect to all the subjects they embrace." Similar expressions of praise from printed sources could be multiplied, but it must suffice to quote from the preface to the fourteenth edition of the Commentaries edited by John M. Gould, where after the lapse of sixty years, the opinions of Kent's contemporaries are verified. "The masterpiece of Chancellor Kent," he says, "has now become so interwoven with judicial decisions that these commentaries upon our frame of government and system of laws will doubtless continue to rank as the first of American legal classics so long as the present order shall prevail. It is worthy of note that, in the preparation of this edition, notwithstanding the rapid development and extension of doctrine in our growing country, the statements of this jurist, though long since made, have rarely been found criticised or curtailed in final decisions."

While the literary and judicial output already mentioned, together with a great amount of general and special reading and a constant and growing correspondence, would appear to have been evidence of a busy life of painstaking industry, it is not to be supposed that the decisions from the bench and the successive editions of the Commentaries are the only remains of Kent's scholarship. In 1801, with Radcliffe he published in two volumes the Revised Laws of New York. In the later years of his life he delivered a number of notable addresses which were published; and he edited an edition of the Charter of New York City (1836), accompanied by a treatise on the powers and duties of the Mayor and other municipal officers. He retained his interest in general reading to the last day of his life, and was considered such an authority that in August, 1840, he was asked by the president of the New York Mercantile Library Association to prepare a list of books for the guidance of members in supplementing their formal education. The list of sixty-nine pages was published in 1840, and reprinted with additions in 1853. He continued to act as office counsel, and divided his declining years between work, reading, writing, and the enjoyment of life with his family. He notes with pride that in 1841 his son William became a judge of the New York Supreme Court, and that in July, 1846, he was appointed Professor of Law at Harvard College in succession to Judge Story. His ten last summers were spent at a cottage in Essex County, New Jersey, and his winters in New York. He died in New York, on December 12, 1847, at the age of eighty-four, surrounded by his family, and leaving the wife whom he had married when she was sixteen, and who had been his partner for sixty-three years. Until the hour of his death he suffered no serious illness, and his declining days were peaceful and contented, though still active. A picture of his life at this time is given in a letter that he wrote to Daniel Webster on December 21, 1842:[7] "I am indeed in my eightieth year," he says, "but thank God I am wonderfully well and active, and my ardor for reading, and my sensibilities are, I think, as alive as ever to the charms of nature, of literature, and society. . . . My reading is regular and constant; all the reports of law decisions, as fast as I can procure them, all the periodicals, foreign and domestic, and old literature and new books, are steadily turned over. . . . I partly ride and partly walk down town daily to my office, and have occasional opinions to give, but more out of the State than in it, and then hasten up to my attractive home and office on Union Square, facing the lofty *jet d'eau,* which is constantly playing before my eyes. The associations with this water are to me delightful. I was born on my father's farm in Putnam County in the eastern part of the Highlands, and that farm was bound-

[7] Writings and Speeches of Daniel Webster, 18: 160–162.

ed east on the Croton River, where I used to fish and swim in my youthful days. God bless the stream! How would it have astonished my parents if they had been foretold, in 1770, that their eldest son would live in the midst of the city of New York with that very Croton pouring its pure and living waters through the streets and throwing its majestic columns of water fifty-six feet into the air. So you see how charmingly I am enabled in my evening days *ducere solicito jocunda obtura vito.*"

EDWARD LIVINGSTON

CHAPTER VII

Edward Livingston and His System of Penal Law

Of men possessed of ideals to which they unalterably adhere throughout long lives filled with notable and distracting events, there is no more conspicuous example than Edward Livingston. Although he achieved national fame as an advocate, legislator and executive, and international renown as a cabinet member and diplomatist, his permanent reputation rests on an accomplishment not directly connected with any of the public events of his life. For his career in the service of his country there is warrant for applying to him such words of characterization as patriot and statesman; and although he was so considered, both during his life and afterwards, yet he was also held up to scorn as a common defaulter, a person false to a public trust and a traitor. For years he was engaged in a lawsuit of peculiar popular interest and in a public controversy with no less an adversary than the President of the United States. With a tenacity of purpose, a legal knowledge and clearsightedness, and a dignified pugnacity almost unexampled, he surmounted all impediments, won over even his enemies, and rose to a position second only to that of the Presidency. These events of his life form a story that must be briefly told in order that we may understand the circumstances under which he produced a great constructive work of legal literature, the "System of Penal Law for the State of Louisiana."

Coming of Scotch ancestry, he was born at Clermont,

Columbia County, New York, May 26, 1764. His elder brother was Robert R. Livingston, the first Chancellor of New York State. He entered Princeton College as a junior in 1779, and was graduated in 1781, one of a class of five. In Albany, New York, for three years he studied law with Judge Lansing. Two years later, in New York City, he was admitted to practice, January, 1785, thus becoming an associate at the Bar of Burr, Hamilton, Benson, Troup and Kent. For three successive terms beginning in 1796 he was elected member of Congress from New York, and then, in 1801, at the age of thirty-seven, he became Mayor of New York City. At the same time he was appointed by President Jefferson United States Attorney for the District of New York. It was not then considered objectionable for a person to hold two public offices at the same time. As head of the city government he presided over the Mayor's Court, rendering decisions which he collected in a volume of reports,[1] which among New York reports were preceded in point of time only by Coleman's Cases.

In connection with the office of United States District Attorney, he now suffered the first touch of adversity, the misappropriation by a subordinate of nearly $44,000 of the fees paid into the office. This was in the year 1803, when yellow fever broke out in New York. During the epidemic, Livingston devoted himself, both in the capacity of Mayor, and personally, to the relief of the stricken, until he became himself a victim of the disease. When he recovered, the defalcation was made known to him. He immediately conveyed all of his property to a trustee to be sold for the benefit of the Government in

[1] Judicial opinions delivered in the Mayor's Court of the City of New York in the year 1802. New York, D. Longworth, 1803.

the liquidation of his liability, and resigned both of his offices. There seems to be no doubt that Livingston had been negligent in the administration of the finances of his office, although none of the missing funds had passed through his own hands. He had failed properly to protect the public property entrusted to him by virtue of his office. He acknowledged his liability and was overwhelmed by the catastrophe which seemed likely to put a period to his career. Eventually the debt was paid in full, both principal and interest, but this did not occur until 1826, when his indebtedness amounted to more than $100,000. Although the mismanagement of his office may now be looked upon as an incident of a life otherwise beyond reproach, and although it disclosed a constitutional inability with regard to financial matters for which no excuse can be made, the event led up to the most notable accomplishment of his life. Without it he probably would have lacked the opportunity for preparing and publishing his Code.

It was just at this period that Louisiana was purchased by the United States, and Livingston's attention was specially drawn to the new country by the fact that his brother Robert was then minister to France. Being skilled in the Civil Law by virtue of special study, and stirred by the possibility of quickly retrieving his fortunes in the land of promise, Livingston set out for what he confidently believed would be a residence of only a few years in New Orleans. His wife having died, his children were left with relatives in New York. Arriving on February 7, 1804, after a voyage of six and one-half weeks, he immediately began the practice of law. In June, 1805, he married a second time. His affairs began to prosper, when, in 1806, an accusation was made against him which came near to being his undoing. He was charged by General James Wilkinson, Senior Officer of the United States Army and Governor of Upper Louisiana, with complicity in the revolutionary schemes of Aaron Burr. The chief evidence upon which Wilkinson based his charges was a direct result of Livingston's financial incompetency. The transfer to the Government of his property in New York had left his private debts unliquidated. After his emigration to New Orleans, a judgment had been entered against him, which was assigned by the judgment creditor to Burr, who in turn gave to Dr. Bollman, a resident of New Orleans, a draft for $1,500 on Livingston. This transaction seemed to Wilkinsôn to connect both Bollman and Livingston with Burr's enterprise. His suspicion was strengthened when, on the arrest of Bollman, the latter engaged Livingston as counsel. Then, during proceedings for a writ of habeas corpus, in open court, Wilkinson accused Livingston of misprision of treason. Livingston denied the accusation and demanded that it be made in writing under oath, but Wilkinson refused. Although there was no foundation for the charge, there was grave danger that it might be pressed because Livingston was then, on account of his neglect of duty in New York, in the disfavor of President Jefferson. Livingston was never arrested, and was completely exonerated by the acquittal of Bollman, who had been taken to Washington for trial; but the unfortunate affair did not tend to raise him in the estimation of President Jefferson, and it also made a portion of the local population ready to believe ill of him.

The Batture Controversy

When Livingston began the practice of law in New Orleans he found no dearth of business, but that little money was in circulation. Some of his fees were therefore paid by the transfer of the title to real estate. One of his clients was John Gravier, who owned land along the river front near the city. His property was protected from the spring freshets by a levee, and between this levee and low-water mark was a strip of alluvial land known as the Batture St. Marie. It had long been used by the populace for the storage of wood, and by fishermen as a landing place. Livingston advised Gravier that this strip belonged to the owners of the abutting property, and Gravier thereupon transferred to Livingston by deed a part of the Batture. Gravier then sued the city of New Orleans for confirmation of a quiet title. This was in 1805. Two years later (May 23, 1807) judgment was rendered by the Superior Court of the Territory of Orleans in favor of Gravier.[2] Livingston then entered upon his part of the property and began to improve it by digging a canal for ships. Trouble immediately ensued; the people objected to being excluded from the use of the Batture; and a presentment was made to the Grand Jury that Livingston's improvements constituted a nuisance, that there was danger of the harbor being filled up by change of the river's current, and that the people had a prescriptive right to store wood on the Batture and remove soil from it. The presentment was not followed up; but Livingston's laborers were driven off by the populace, and as often led back by the owner.

[2] John Gravier v. Mayor, Aldermen and Inhabitants of the City of New Orleans, Am. Law Journal, 2: 441–443.

Governor Claiborne, who was appealed to for military protection, referred the whole matter to the Federal Government, and sent Colonel Macarty as messenger to suggest that the Batture belonged to the United States, and that they were not divested of title by the decision of the Territorial Court. President Jefferson and his Cabinet deliberated on the question, and his Attorney General gave it as his opinion that Livingston was an intruder on Government property, under the act of March 3, 1807 (3 St. Large, Ch. 91). The Secretary of State instructed the United States Marshal at New Orleans (Nov. 30, 1807) to use his civil power to remove all persons from the Batture; and the Secretary of War gave orders to the commanding officer at New Orleans to use military force if requested by the Governor. The Marshal then removed Livingston from possession, and the latter obtained a court order restraining the Marshal. This order was disregarded.

With the action of the Federal Executive in conflict with the decision of the Territorial Court of last resort, and with Livingston dispossessed of the Batture, now began a legal controversy which continually grew in complexity and which involved many notable personages. The suits which grew out of it became popularly known as the Batture cases, filling many pages of the Louisiana Reports. The attorneys for the City of New Orleans shifted their ground. The case was newly stated by both contestants and submitted to attorneys for opinions, which were written and published at length. Those of Derbigny and Thierry were for the City; those of Du Ponceau, Ingersoll, Rawle, Tilghman and Lewis, for Livingston. These were gathered together and published in

Hall's American Law Journal.[3] Meanwhile, Jefferson had laid the whole matter before Congress in a special message (March 7, 1808). Livingston answered by an "Address to the people of the United States," but Congress never took cognizance of the controversy. On March 4, 1809, Jefferson retired to private life, whereupon a new chapter in the controversy began. Livingston, in the United States Circuit Court for the District of Virginia, brought action in *trespass quare clausum fregit* against Jefferson as a private person and not as a public official. Jefferson demurred to the jurisdiction and to the form of the declaration, and pleaded that he had ordered the expulsion of Livingston in the capacity of President and not as an individual. The court then dismissed the suit for want of jurisdiction, Chief Justice Marshall concurring in the opinion of Justice Tyler.[4] The latter, father of President Tyler, prefaced his opinion with the following: "While I freely acknowledge how much I was pleased with the ingenuity and eloquence of the plaintiff's counsel, I cannot do so much injustice to plain truth, as to say that any conviction was wrought on my mind, of the soundness of the arguments they exhibited in a legal acceptation. It is the happy talent of some professional gentlemen, and particularly of the plaintiff's counsel, often to make 'the worse appear the better cause;' but it is the duty of the judge to guard against the effects intended to be produced, by selecting those arguments and principles from the mass afforded as will enable him to give such an opinion at least, as may satisfy himself, if not others.

[3] Am. Law Journal, 2:282–358; 392–455.

[4] Livingston v. Jefferson, Am. Law Journal, 4:78–87; 15 Fed. Cas. 660–665.

These arguments and this eloquence, however, have been met by an Herculean strength of forensic ability, which, I take pride in saying, sheds lustre over the Bar of Virginia." The decision of the Virginia Court did not go to the merits of the controversy, which was now carried up to the Court of Public Opinion. In preparation for the Virginia suit, Jefferson, from his retreat in Monticello, had prepared a statement of the case for use of counsel. It is dated July 31, 1810. After the decision of the case, this statement was published in New York (1812), and this publication led the editor of the American Law Journal, who was frankly favorable to Livingston, to print a counter argument which had been prepared by Du Ponceau in February, 1809.[5] In a subsequent volume, Jefferson's tract with additional notes by the author was published in 1814,[6] accompanied by Livingston's answer prepared in July, 1813.[7]

Both statements are models of controversial literature, as would be expected from the author of the Declaration of Independence on the one hand, and on the other, from a legal and forensic advocate so skilled as Livingston. The arguments were largely based on citations of Roman, French and Spanish law, a field in which Livingston was superior to Jefferson. He was, however, at a disadvantage in an argument with the former Chief Magistrate of the United States, who could with impunity refer to Livingston as "an eagle-eyed adversary," a "greedy individual," and one who, in view of his well-known financial difficulties, "could not suddenly forget the fleshpots of Egypt, even in the land

[5] Am. Law Journal, 4: 517–562.
[6] *Ibid.*, 5: vii–xii, 1–91.
[7] *Ibid.*, 5: 105–299.

of Canaan." In such a controversy there is no means of awarding the victory. Chancellor Kent, however, believed that it had been won by Livingston. "If I had any doubt of your title to the Batture after reading Jefferson's pamphlet," he wrote, "your reply has completely removed it. . . . Permit me to assure you that I have sympathized with you throughout the whole of the controversy, as I took a very early impression that you was cruelly and shamefully persecuted, and that, too, by the executive authority of the United States. I am more and more confirmed in this opinion, and Mr. Jefferson has richly merited all the reproach and indignation which your pamphlet conveys. . . . This last pamphlet is the ablest work with which you have hitherto obliged the public, and it gives you new and increasing claims to their consideration.[8]

In the meantime, Livingston had not neglected judicial remedies. It will be remembered that in 1807, Livingston had obtained an order of Court restraining the United States Marshal from removing him from the Batture, and that, disregarding this order and obedient to the Federal authorities, Livingston had been dispossessed. He now brought suit against the Marshal in the United States District Court for the Territory of Orleans, according to the forms of the Civil Law, to obtain damages for the expulsion and to be restored to possession. The defendant pleaded the warrant of the President as his justification, but after argument, the Court, on August 4, 1813, decided that the warrant was illegal, being unauthorized by the act under which it was issued, and directed that the plaintiff should be restored to posses-

[8] Kent to Livingston, May 13, 1814, printed in Hunt, Life of Edward Livingston, pp. 181–182.

sion, which was accordingly done. This seemed a victory for Livingston, although ultimately it was robbed of most of its substantial benefits. It was in fact the prelude to a series of suits involving the Batture in which Livingston lost most of the financial advantages of possession. The chief of these suits were decided in 1819[9] adversely to the defendant. But still there remained matter for litigation by which in 1826, when he was approaching the height of his political career, Livingston succeeded in disentangling some lots which had formed part of the original Batture. These lots he offered to the United States Treasury Department in satisfaction of his debt. The offer was accepted, and the obligation canceled by a Marshal's sale on execution, the United States becoming purchaser through an agent. The judgment was for $100,014.89, representing the original debt with interest. Later the Government sold the lots for $106,208.08.

Meanwhile, Livingston's reputation as a statesman and jurist had been steadily growing. He participated in the Battle of New Orleans, serving as adviser to General Andrew Jackson, whom he already knew as a fellow member of Congress, thus cementing a friendship which lasted to the end of his life. In 1820 he was elected a member of the Louisiana lower house. In July, 1822, he was unanimously elected a member of the United States House of Representatives from the New Orleans district, taking his seat in December, 1823. He was twice re-elected, serving with Randolph, Clay and Webster. While in Washington, he practised law before the United States Supreme Court. In 1828, Jackson was elected President, and Livingston United States Senator from

[9] Morgan v. Livingston, 6 Mart. (O. S.) 19; Gravier v. Livingston, 6 Mart. (O. S.) 281.

Louisiana. In 1831, Jackson appointed him Secretary of State, and he took office on May 24, when he was sixty-seven years old. Two years later, May, 1833, he was appointed Envoy Extraordinary and Minister Plenipotentiary at Paris. In France, he handled the delicate situation arising out of the failure of the French Chamber of Deputies to appropriate the money needed to pay the indemnity due the United States for French spoliations under the Berlin and Milan Decrees. The claims had been acknowledged by Louis Philippe in the Treaty of July 4, 1831. Finally, when the appropriation was made, but coupled with a proviso which he deemed inconsistent with the dignity of the United States, he demanded his passports, and arrived home on June 23, 1835. He died on May 23, 1836.

The System of Penal Law

If the above brief sketch were filled out with important details, there would appear to be no place left in so busy a life for pursuing a purpose demanding the best thought of the best of minds. Yet for forty-three years, in adversity, debt, litigation, engrossed in the cares of public office, even in the height of success, he worked incessantly at the problem of improving the system of penal laws in the United States. The result was a work which Villemain declared to be "without example from the hand of any one man," and Livingston's name will ever be coupled with those of Bentham and Field as one of the three great codifiers.

The germ of Livingston's interest in penal law is found in a resolution which he introduced in the House of Representatives on December 15, 1795, "that a committee be appointed to inquire and report whether any and what alterations should be made in the penal laws of the United States, by substituting milder punishments for certain crimes, for which infamous and capital punishments are now inflicted."[10] The committee was appointed with Livingston as chairman. To assist in this inquiry, Livingston, on December 31, 1795,[11] introduced a resolution calling on the President of the United States to cause the House "to be furnished with an account of the number of convictions for crimes, that have taken place under the penal laws of the United States, specifying the crime, the date and place of conviction and the sentence." On December 19, 1796,[12] the House passed, on Livingston's initiative, another resolution similar in purpose to that of December 15, 1795. Livingston was again made chairman; but no tangible result came from these resolutions. The failure of this first effort might perhaps have dampened Livingston's ardor, if it had not been for the influence of Jeremy Bentham. Referring to the experience, in a letter of August 10, 1829, written to Bentham from New York,[13] Livingston said, "It is more than thirty years ago that, then representing this city in the House of Representatives of the United States, I made an ineffectual attempt to mitigate the severity of our penal laws. The perusal of your works, edited by Dumont, fortified me in a design to prosecute the subject, whenever a fit occasion should offer." In a later letter (July 1, 1830), Livingston gave further acknowledgment to Bentham:[14] "Although strongly impressed with the

[10] Annals of Congress, Dec. 15, 1795.
[11] House Journal, 2: 394.
[12] House Journal, 2: 624.
[13] Works: Bowring ed. 11: 23.
[14] Works: Bowring ed. 11: 51.

defects of our actual system of penal law," he wrote, "yet the perusal of your works first gave method to my ideas, and taught me to consider legislation as a science governed by certain principles applicable to all its different branches, instead of an occasional exercise of power called forth only on particular occasions, without relation to, or connexion with, each other."

In 1803, while Mayor of New York, he communicated to the Mechanic Society a plan to form an organization to give employment to strangers, to citizens who through sickness or misfortune had lost their positions, to widows and orphans, and to discharged or pardoned convicts. A chief reason which he urged was the prevention of mendacity and crime, and the reformation of those who have already suffered punishment. Thus he foreshadowed that attitude toward discharged prisoners which has received so much attention of late. "The odium justly attached to the crime," he said, "is continued to the culprit after he has suffered its penalty; he is restored to society, but prejudice repels him from its bosom; he has acquired the skill and has the inclination to provide honestly for his support. Years of penitence and labor have wiped away his crime, and given him habits of industry, and skill to direct them. But no means are provided for their execution. He has no capital of his own, and that of others will not be entrusted to him; he is not permitted to labor; he dares not beg; and he is forced for subsistence to plunge anew into the same crimes, to suffer the same punishment he has just undergone, or, perhaps, with more caution and address, to escape it. Thus the institution, instead of diminishing, may increase the number of offenses." [15]

[15] Hunt: Life, p. 95.

When Livingston began the practice of law in New Orleans, the Territory was in process of organizing its judicial system. No code of practice had been adopted, and there was much confusion in existing practice on account of conflicting systems of law. He, therefore, suggested that the rules be simplified, and he was appointed by Governor Claiborne to draw up the new rules. This he did in a single act of twenty-two sections filling only twenty-six pages. It was passed by the Legislative Council of the Territory of Orleans at its first session and approved by the Governor, April 10, 1805.[16] It is entitled "An act regulating the practice of the Superior Court, in civil causes." It was so simple that, according to Livingston, it could be mastered in a single day. In a letter to Jeremy Bentham, written July 1, 1830, he described it as being "based upon the plan of requiring each party to state, in intelligible language, the cause of complaint and the grounds of defense. I comprised it in a single law of a few pages; and although, from its novelty, many questions may be naturally supposed to arise under it, before the court and suitors become accustomed to its provisions; yet our books of Reports, from 1808 to 1823, contain fewer cases depending on disputed points of practice than occurred in a single year, 1803, in New York, where they proceed according to the English law, which has been in a train of settlements by adjudication so many hundred years.[17]

Although this law had to do with civil procedure, it may be considered a step in the development of Livingston's interest in codification, and an indication of his

[16] Acts passed at the first session of the Legislative Council, Chap. 26, pp. 210–260, printed in parallel pages of French and English.

[17] Bentham: Works. Bowring ed. 11:52.

attitude toward simplification of legal processes; and this experience led, after he became a member of the Louisiana Legislature in 1820, to his appointment as one of a Committee of "three jurisconsults" to revise the Civil Code of the State.[18] This Committee finished its work in 1824 when its revised Code was for the most part adopted by the Legislature.[19] Before this time, Livingston had been elected to Congress; but he was active in drawing up the plan for the Code, and unsuccessfully attempted to engraft on the scheme a device which later was advocated also by Bentham. The latter, writing to Livingston, February 23, 1830,[20] proposed to prevent written codes from "being clouded and covered over by an overgrowth of judge-made law," by requiring judges to adhere to the letter of the law, and bring about changes in it only by framing amendments which they would be required to transmit to the Legislature. "I think I understand the outline of your plan for the gradual amelioration of a written code, without the aid of judicial decisions, and thus obviating one of the strongest objections that is made to a system of written law," wrote Livingston in reply on July 1, 1830,[21] "but I should wish exceedingly to see the outline filled up, for I feel some pride in having made a similar proposal in relation to our Civil Code in the year 1823. . . . You will find it from page eight to the end of a short report which I enclose. . . . The gentlemen, joined with me in the

[18] Louisiana Acts, 1822, p. 108. Resolution of March 14, 1822.

[19] For a note by A. K. Barbour on this Code and the Code of Practice drawn up at the same time, see Law Library Journal, 13: 69–71.

[20] Bentham: Works. Bowring ed. 11:36.

[21] *Ibid.*, 11:51.

commission, were unfortunately too impatient for the completion of this task to enable them to do the work in the manner we had proposed. I was overruled; and the Civil Code was reported and sanctioned in the form you will now see in the copy sent to you."

Under an act of February 10, 1821,[22] Livingston had already been appointed by the Louisiana Senate and House of Representatives "to prepare and present to the next General Assembly for its consideration, a code of criminal law in both the French and English languages, designating all criminal offenses punishable by law, defining the same in clear and explicit terms, designating the punishment to be inflicted on each, laying down the rules of evidence on trials, directing the whole mode of procedure, and pointing out the duties of the Judicial and Executive officers in the performance of their functions under it." The spirit in which the work was authorized and undertaken is shown by the preamble to the act: "Whereas it is of primary importance in every well-regulated state, that the code of criminal law should be founded on one principle, viz.: the prevention of crime, that all offenses should be clearly and explicitly defined, in language generally understood; that punishment should be proportioned to offenses; that the rules of evidence should be ascertained as applicable to each offense; that the mode of procedure should be simple, and the duty of magistrates, executive officers and individuals assisting them, should be pointed out by law, and whereas the system of criminal law by which this state is now governed, is defective in many or all of the points enumerated, therefore," etc., etc.

[22] La. Acts, 1820–21, pp. 30–32.

Although Livingston was still engaged in litigation arising out of the Batture controversy, he immediately set to work on the Code. At the next session of the Assembly he reported his whole plan which was approved by resolution, earnestly soliciting him to prosecute the work, and ordering the publication of 2,000 copies of the report with annexed draft of the projected Code.[23] Before the Code was ready for the printer, he was elected a member of Congress and took his seat in December, 1823. During the session, he had little leisure to complete the work, but at the close of the long session, which ended in May, 1824, he repaired to New York City with his family to spend the recess between the first and the second sessions. Here, at number 66 Broadway, he completed the Code, and here he experienced a catastrophe which would have overwhelmed a lesser man. He was now sixty-one years old, and although an honored member of Congress, still in debt for an ever-increasing amount to the Government which he served. But his most cherished wish was about to be realized,—the publication of his System of Penal Law, for which his life had been a preparation, and which was the product of nearly four years of intense intellectual application. What happened may best be told in his own words. Writing to his friend Du Ponceau, who was his counsel in the Batture controversy, on November 16, 1824, he said: "The night before last, I wrote you an apologetic letter, accounting for not having before that time thanked you for your letter and your book. My excuse lay before me, in four Codes: of Crimes and Punishments, of Criminal Procedure, of Prison Discipline, and of Evidence. This was about one o'clock; I retired to rest, and

[23] Resolution, March 21, 1822, La. Acts, 1822, pp. 108–110.

in about three hours was waked by the cry of fire. It had broken out in my writing room, and, before it was discovered, not a vestige of my work remained, except about fifty or sixty pages which were at the printer's, and a few very imperfect notes in another place. You may imagine, for you are an author, my dismay on perceiving the evidence of this calamity; for circumstanced as I am, it is a real one. My habits for some years past, however, have fortunately inured me to labor, and my whole life has to disappointment and distress. I, therefore, bear it with more fortitude than I otherwise should, and, instead of repining, work all night and correct proof all day, to repair the loss and get the work ready by the time I had promised it to the Legislature." [24] Six days after the catastrophe, he again wrote to Du Ponceau:—"I thank you most sincerely for your kind participation in my calamity, for although I put the best face upon it, I cannot help feeling it as such. I have always found occupation the best remedy for distress of every kind. The great difficulty I have found on those occasions was to rally the energies of the mind, so as to bring them to undertake it. Here, exertion was necessary not only to enable me to bear the misfortune, but to repair it; and I, therefore, did not lose an hour. The very night after the accident, I sat up until three o'clock, with a determination to keep pace with my printer; hitherto I have succeeded, and he has, with what is already printed, copy for an hundred pages of the Penal Code. I find my recollection strengthens by keeping the attention fixed on one subject, and that by the help of my loose notes, which serve as *jalons* (have we any English word for this?), I find my old route easier than I expected. Next week,

[24] Hunt: Life, pp. 291–292.

about Saturday, I will send you the Penal Code; but you cannot judge fairly of it without the other codes, each of which elucidates and supplies deficiencies in the others. The part I shall find most difficult to replace is the preliminary discourse, of which I have not a single note, and with which (I may confide it to your friendly ear) I was satisfied. A composition of that kind depends so much upon the feeling of the moment in which it is written, the disposition that suggests not only the idea but the precise word that is proper to express it is so evanescent (mine at least are), that it will, I fear, be utterly impossible for me to regain it." [25]

His efforts were successful to the extent of immediately rewriting, and publishing, his Penal Code and Code of Procedure, the former in 1824 and the latter in 1825. The project for the Code had already been published in London, in 1824, at the expense of Dr. Southwood Smith.[26] Funds for the publication of the whole system were appropriated by the Louisiana Legislature, on January 25, 1825.[27] The Code of Evidence was not, however, rewritten and published until 1830.[28]

Thus we find Livingston in 1826 with two causes for rejoicing; first, the partial publication of his Code, and second, the cancelation of his debt, the circumstances of which have already been recounted. Moreover he was a member of the United States House of Representatives and in line for further preferment by the United States Government. But he did not relinquish his endeavors for the improvement of the penal system of the United

[25] Hunt: Life, pp. 292–293.
[26] See Bentham: Works, 11:35–36.
[27] La. Acts, 7th Leg. (1824–25) p. 46.
[28] Bentham: Works, 11:23, 35–36.

States. On the contrary he prepared and presented to the House of Representatives "a system of penal laws for the United States" which was printed by order of the House in 1828.

After he took his seat in the United States Senate in December, 1829, he further followed up his project. He was interested in a bill introduced on February 16, 1831, providing for the preparation of a system of civil and criminal law for the District of Columbia;[29] and on March 3, of the same year, he brought in a bill[30] to rehabilitate his scheme for a complete system of penal law for the United States. He points out two distinctive features of his plan; first, the total abolition of the death penalty; and second, the defining and punishing, by positive law, of "offenses against the laws of nations, and among them some which had hitherto been left without any sanction, such as offenses against the law which regulates, in modern times, the conduct of civilized nations with respect to each other in time of war as well as of peace."

Not until 1833 was there any complete publication of Livingston's System. In that year it was issued in Philadelphia. A French edition appeared in Paris, 1872, and the "Complete Works of Edward Livingston on Criminal Jurisprudence" were published in New York, by the National Prison Association, in 1873. For fourteen years, from 1822 to 1836, the adoption of the plan, in whole or in part, by the various jurisdictions of the United States and by foreign governments, was advocated by Livingston. His System was revolutionary in character, and therefore had ardent adherents and violent

[29] Register of Debates in Congress, 7:209, 211.
[30] *Ibid.*, 7:343–344.

opponents. It challenged the attention of the foremost thinkers of the world. Of the fact that the first issue of 1824–1825 was read with care and for the most part with approval by Chancellor Kent, there is the best evidence. In the Columbia University Law Library is a copy of the book presented to Kent by Livingston. The extensive notes in the former's handwriting, on sheets of paper inserted at the back of the volume, show not only the creative character of the publication, but are also good examples of Kent's method of study. For these reasons, some excerpts from Kent's notes are now for the first time printed at the end of this chapter.

It would be futile to attempt systematically to describe the substance of Livingston's Penal System in so brief a sketch as the present. It will be understood from what has already been said that it was not merely legalistic. It was intended to be what has in recent years been called "social legislation" for the prevention of crime, the reformation of the criminal, and the protection of society, and in no case merely for vengeance. For instance, if the Code had been adopted, the death penalty would have been abolished, and imprisonment for life at hard labor substituted. And for a warning to others, the following ceremonies would have attended the sentence: "When sentence is pronounced for murder," says the Code of Procedure, "the seat and table of the court shall be hung in black, and the prisoner shall, immediately after the sentence is pronounced, be enveloped in a black mantle that shall cover his whole body, with a cowl or veil drawn over his head; and shall be thus conveyed in a cart, hung with black, to the place of his confinement." Such proposals as these appealed to the imagination; in some cases excited ridicule. But each detail of the System was an integral part of the whole, and the theory of each of the four Codes was explained in a series of introductory reports. Of the latter, a reviewer said in 1836:[31] "No one can fail to be impressed especially with the enlightened spirit of philanthropy, the single aim to benefit his fellow creatures, which breathes throughout these discussions; and to this it may be added, that there is always an unaffected beauty and simplicity in the language, frequently rising, when the topic demands it, to a fervent eloquence, which will command the attention and interest of those who might be repelled by the gravity and want of imagination, with which such subjects are generally treated." Moreover, Livingston's fundamental concepts have stood the test of time. Writing in 1902,[32] Eugene Smith states what may be taken to be the modern view of Livingston's work. "Seventy-five years have since elapsed," he wrote, "and yet it is probably safe now to say that these Codes embody the most comprehensive and enlightened system of criminal law that has ever been presented to the world. They constitute a thesaurus from which the world has ever since been drawing ideas and principles. The Code of Reform and Prison Discipline is especially striking from the breadth of its view, and in some particulars its wisdom is yet in advance of even the present age."

Livingston's Codes were never formally adopted in any jurisdiction in the United States. The Code of Reform and Prison Discipline was, however, in 1834, adopted word for word by Guatemala; and even in Livingston's lifetime there were many evidences of the influential character of his work. Among others, Jeremy Bentham, Vic-

[31] North American Review, 43: 305–6.
[32] Columbia Law Review, 2: 32.

tor Hugo, Lafayette, Story, Marshall, Madison and Kent wrote him letters of approval. Even Jefferson wrote him appreciative letters. The King of Sweden and the Emperor of Russia sent him autograph letters. He was chosen Foreign Associate of the Institute of France; and at Geneva, on a monument consecrated "to the inviolability of the life of man," his name was placed over the inscription, "Il demanda l'abolition de la peine de mort a l'Amerique."

After his return from France, from whence he came in June, 1835, upon the frigate *Constitution,* at the conclusion of his mission as ambassador, Livingston retired to Montgomery Place to spend his remaining years. But his activity in legal affairs continued, for in January, 1836, he argued a case in the United States Supreme Court in Washington, with Daniel Webster as junior associate, and Benjamin F. Butler, Attorney General, as opponent. The winter of 1835–1836 he spent in New York.

Up to the last days of his life, he continued to work on his Codes, for on March 16, 1836, he wrote the following letter to Chancellor Kent:

"Here my good friend is the work I mentioned to you yesterday. At an hour when there is nothing more important to require your attention, may I ask your observations on that part which defines the offenses of conspiracy, insurrection, and treason, and particularly on the division of the latter crime into two classes. That the opposition, even by an armed force, to a particular, and perhaps oppressive law, should be classed with and incur the same penalty with the traitorous co-operation with the enemies of our country in their attempts to subjugate it or to open rebellion for the overthrow by force of arms, of its Constitution and laws, appeared to me cruel absurdity; and that founded, as it is, on mere construction it might be avoided without a breach of the Constitution. I have a strong belief that the provisions I have introduced have effected this. Your opinion will confirm or shake this confidence.

"Do not conclude that I had the vanity to direct the lettering on the back of the volume; it was bound as well as printed by order of the House of Representatives, who placed a few copies at my disposal.

"Very truly & with the highest respect & esteem.

"Your Friend & Obt. Servt

"EDW. LIVINGSTON."

This letter is inserted in a copy of the System of Penal Law for the United States (1828), which is in the Columbia University Law Library inscribed "From the author, to his old and highly respected friend, James Kent." In the same volume the following words were written by Kent:—

"Mr. Livingston died at his Residence at Red Hook on the Hudson Monday May 23d, 1836, by reason of drinking cold water when very warm on Saturday preceding. The weather had ranged from 82 to 86 on Sat. Sunday & Monday. He must have been 72 years of age & upwards, for he was admitted atty. of the Supreme Court in October 1784, & in June 1786 he & I tried a Cause together at the Dutchess circuit."

Excerpts from Kent's Notes on the Penal Code[33]

(1) *Introductory Title*

The objects of the Legislature in establishing the penal

[33] Kent's spelling, punctuation, underlining, etc., have, as far as possible, been followed.

code, & the fundamental Principles & Truths which ought to pervade & govern it are admirably expressed in the Preamble, & with perfect Perspicuity & Precision. p. 2–7.

I object to the too great restriction on the Power of Pardon at pa. 6.

Query? I do not see why the Legislature have not a right to pass a law for the observance of the *Lord's day,* as they have to appoint a general Fast or Thanksgiving Day, and yet the Code at p. 6, 7, would seem to admit the one power & deny the other. Both are allowable on the Principle of moral Instruction & public Good.

This Volume is the *Penal Code.* The *Code of Criminal Procedure* is by itself. The *Code of Prison Discipline* & the *Code of Evidence* I have not seen. p. 8.

Penal Code

(2) *Book 1.—General Provisions*

p. 12. no *constructive* offenses, nothing is punishable but what is forbidden by the *letter* of the law.

p. 14. all final Judgments *with the reasons* to be entered at large on the minutes.

p. 13, 14, ch. 2. The *general Provisions relative to Prosecutions & Trials,* are exceedingly well expressed.

p. 15. I doubt whether Persons under 9 are to be absolutely exempted from penal law. Query?

ch. 3. of *Persons amenable to the Code.* I have examined it carefully, & I think it well drawn & unexceptionable.

ch. 5. The definitions of Principals, accomplices & accessories are admirable. p. 21 etc.

(3) *Book 2. of Offences & Punishments*

ch. 1. The definition & decision of offences is well done. Punishment is only (1) to deprive the Party of the means & desire to repeat the offence, (2) to deter others. p. 4.

Query? is then Imprisonment *penal* or *Punishment* ch. 2. of *Punishments.* They are all either fines, Imprisonment or forfeiture of civil rights. pa. 26, 27.

Query? Is not pecuniary fines condemnable as much as any other forfeiture of Property.

Query? p. 29. The civil right of bearing arms in the Militia or serving on Juries is taken away as a Punishment. Is there any Punishment in the case?

Query? may there not be a levying war against one State without a levying war against the Union—p. 32.

—Query? p. 36. Is not the law too severe, in making it penal for an Executive officer to receive gratuitously extra pay for *Services* required to be done by his office.

—Query? p. 38. may not a Judge *receive a Gift* not from a Suitor, nor a Person in reference to any judicial act—Query? too severe.

—Query? art. p. 40. too severe in many respects & dangerous.

—Query? p. 40. abominable to inhibit Judges from vesting their money in any Bank or Insurance Company.

Page 41. I like the check on Publications concerning cases before Trial.

ch. 2, 4, 6, p. 41–45. defining offences against officers of Justice in Execution of duty & rescue & Breach of Prison, etc. is admirably & most precisely & accurately done.

Query? does not the Author lay too much Stress on depriving a Party of *political rights* as a Punishment? It is everywhere in the Code prescribed as a Punishment.

Query? ch. 8. p. 46. is not a Breach of Duty in an atty. too severely punished as a *public offence.* If being engaged & consulted (supposing nothing material and his client refuse to pay him & abscond etc.) ought there not to be more *discretion* in the Court. The laws of this Code are too inflexible. That is a great Error.

ch. 11—I condemn *in toto* the abolition of Proceedings for *Contempt,* & that all Contempts must be tried by Jury upon Indictment or Information. It is horrible to refer to the Jury to decide what is indecorous or insulting language to the Court. Besides there is no Provision for insulting *Gestures or actions or looks.* The ch. provides only for offences by *words, clamor, noise, violence,* & *threats.* p. 51, 2.

Besides the Judge must at the Trial sit & bear all this *until* Indictment & Trial which may be six months after ! ! !

Tit. 6. ch. 1. *Unlawful assemblies & riots* well defined. But p. 55. suppose a Party does not retire from the assembly within the half hour, because he is sick, lame or afraid, may not the Equity of the case be examined, or must the letter of the law prevail. Query?

Tit. 8. p. 60. I am against the whole of that title. The Press is too wanton already.

May I not tell B. that he is writing freely against Judges of Courts & Persons, & I will not indorse for him any longer if he goes on in that Course—suppose he is my son, is that an offence, because it will injure his *Credit?*

May not a Judge tell his clerk who holds his appointment at his Pleasure, if you keep pouring out your Libels weekly and daily against what is done in. Court I will remove you from the office of Clerk or Register,—am I to be punished for a public offence? ! ! !

p. 84. the Punishment of maliciously administering deleterious drugs to another, though not with intent to kill, is not severe enough. The Imprisonment cannot go beyond 3 months. It ought to go to years hard labor. Query?

—I like making Seduction under Promise of marriage a public offence—p. 86.—so as to lascivious words with design to insult a female. This is new legislation. I like these new guards to modesty and the sex.

p. 87. I concur in making adultery a public offence under the limitations in ch. 3. tit. 16.

tit. 18. ch. 1, 2, 4, of *defamation* is a very important & able work. It makes it a public offence & guards individuals in an admirable manner, & I now can forgive the prior articles about the Liberty of the Press.

at pa. 96. no offence to defame or caricature religion or the objects of religious faith or Principles, of morals, & yet the liberty of the Press is protected—! Query? I believe the fundamental Principles of religion of more Importance to Society than the liberty of the Press.

tit. 19. ch. 1. on assault & Battery in all its complicated degrees well defined & graduated. An excellent article.

But Query?—the Punishment at p. 106 for disfiguring or maiming with that Intent, as are cutting off the Ear or Nose, not sufficient. The Imprisonment cannot exceed 2 years, whereas the offender ought to be hung.

ch. 5. *Homicide* is well defined & all its varieties—a great & painstaking article.

Punishment of Murder of every kind is hard labor for Life.

ch. 6. of Duels—Punishment for killing is Imprisonment not exceeding 4 years & forfeiture of political rights.—All officers civil & military must take an oath that they have not been engaged in a duel since the Promulgation of the penal code, and that they will not.

Oath of Grand Jurors & public Prosecutors to prosecute & indict for offences against the Duel Act.

Sec. 2. to open a letter without authority made a public offence. Query?

Sec. 4. obtaining Property by false Pretences has some excellent provisions. But the false pretences are pushed very far at p. 149, 150, when you get possession on promise of immediate payment & don't pay or redeliver or when you pay in a check which you say is good & know it is not—query? I am inclined to go the whole length for the sake of fair Dealing.

"Notes on reading the last half of this Volume or Code of criminal Procedure.

Book 1. Of the means of preventing & suppressing offences.

The *Objects of the Code of Procedure* for giving Effect to the Penal Code are stated to be seven, and they are wise & excellent Principles upon which criminal Proceedings should be founded—p. 4, 5.

p. 7.—Persons knowing of an Intention to commit a crime of the first grade, is *bound to inform* under Pain of Imprisonment.

p. 8.—A reward of $50 for giving Information of certain high crimes leading to conviction.

p. 9. An offence for to reproach such an Informer.

p. 12. A Person may be summoned before a Magistrate, merely to receive *admonition*—Query?

p. 18, 19. *Nuisances* may be removed by order in certain cases before conviction.

p. 33—when a Party discharged may be reimprisoned for the same offence but it shall not be deemed *the same cause.*

Mem. This is defining & settling some nice Points in our law.

p. 34. The provision don't apply to Persons imprisoned under the authority of U. S. in cases where the courts have jurisdiction.

Book 2. Of the Mode of prosecuting offences.

P. 47, 8, 9. rules prescribed on executing a *warrant of arrest.*

P. 51, 2. The duty of the Magistrate in *examining and committing the accused.* It is full & excellent.

P. 53, 4. as to bailable & not bailable offences & the Extent of Bail.

P. 60, 1 to 67. The Power & duties of the *Grand-Jury.*—It is a full, clear & excellent detail of their organization, mode of Proceedings & duties. They must confine themselves to the business of the penal law & no expression of opinion on any other subject is admissable.

P. 67 to 71.—on the requisites of a good *Indictment.* An offence begun in one district and completed in another may be laid in either—Indictments for forgery must set forth the written Instrument exactly, but ornamental Engravings need not be imitated.

P. 72–76. The Indictment being served on the deft, he must be brought into court to make *Exceptions* if any so that Informal & inaccurate matter may be corrected, & when he comes to plead & to trial, nothing but the merits can be heard. All matters of form are *amendable.* If the Exceptions be of matter not amendable, the accused may be re-indicted.

P. 80, 1, 2. *Challenges* to Jurors are to the array and to the Polls. Peremptory challenge is only to nine Jurors by Deft. & to three by the Prosecutor. Challenges for cause are numerous as relationship within the 9th degree & Having *formed such an Opinion of the Guilt or Innocence of the Deft. as in the opinion of the Juror himself renders him not impartial.*—Query?

P. 83–88. on *the Trial.* In the charge to the Jury the Judge shall not *recapitulate* the Testimony unless requested by one or more of the Jurors—The Jury may be discharged & a new Trial had, when it appears to the Court that there is no Probability that they will agree, & that the Health of one or more of them will be endangered by confinement.

P. 93–5. *new Trials* may be granted after acquittal in certain cases & after conviction in many more, & among other causes when the Verdict in the Opinion of the Court is *contrary to Evidence*—Query?

P. 99—*awful ceremonies* on giving Sentence in case of murder—Query?

P. 97—Judgt. of Imprisonment as well as of a fine may be awarded *in the absence* of the guilty.

P. 105—Query? the definition of an *Oath*—It is made too broad—an *honorary* engagement is added—Query? a *formule* used as the English of formula.

P. 107—Executive officers need not swear to any act. Their oath of office carries all—Query?

P. 115–119. The duties of Clerk, Interpreter, Reporter & of publishing all Reports of every criminal case in the City Gazette every month etc. *very minutely* prescribed!

P. 126—Proceedings in case of Treasure trove, forbidding the finder to conceal the fact. He must give notice. This is an important chapter & Principle, & it is taken from the civil law.

P. 132—Provisions for paying *Innocent Persons* who had been prosecuted & acquitted. It rests on the discretion of the Judge—a just and excellent Provision.

CHAPTER VIII.

Henry Wheaton

All work and no play did not make Henry Wheaton a dull man, although there is little evidence that he ever devoted himself to those lighter forms of entertainment which are supposed to whet the blades of the intellect. I do not know that anyone has ever described him as precocious, but undoubtedly he was engaged in the pursuits of the grown man at an age when the modern youth is entering college. To graduate at sixteen, delivering a commencement oration on the Progress of the Mathematical and Physical Sciences during the Eighteenth Century; to be admitted to the Bar three years later; and in the same year to translate into English the new Napoleonic Code, is in truth to start early on a serious career. And this beginning was a promise which did not misrepresent the future. Apparently he worked at all times, displaying almost unbelievable industry, coupled with a brilliancy the continuance of which can only be explained by the assumption that he was one of those happy and rare individual persons to whom work is both satisfaction and recreation. It is not surprising therefore that a classmate of Wheaton's at Brown University, John Whipple, writing in 1854, after remarking that no part of Wheaton's life "was distinguished by any of those stirring incidents which most deeply interest the popular mind," adds that "it furnishes a higher lesson, and a more useful example to the young." [1]

[1] MS. letter to William B. Lawrence, preserved in Brown University library.

Henry Wheaton

To hold a man up as an "example to the young," while stating at the same time that his life is devoid of stirring incidents, is perhaps a sure method of creating a prejudice against him as a subject for pleasurable study. To remove this impression, in Wheaton's case, it is necessary only to glance at the events of his life; for without furnishing any romantic or dramatic episodes, his career was one of sustained interest intimately connected with the larger affairs of his time. In fact, he may be said to have been distinguished as a lawyer, editor, historian, diplomat and publicist, and he unquestionably acquired international fame which has not yet subsided. The biography of such a man cannot be compressed into a few pages, nor is that the purpose of the present sketch. His literary works are, however, the expression of the man himself, and their story throws a clearer light upon him than would any formal account. In whatever position, office or country he was, he wrote, losing no opportunity to place the results of his study and observation on the printed page. The story of his writings therefore includes the whole of his life, the events of which now appear, after the lapse of over eighty years, to have been the preparation for writing the works on international law by which his name is most often remembered.[2]

[2] 1785. Born, Providence, R. I.
1802. Graduated, Brown University.
1805. Admitted to Rhode Island Bar.
1812–1815. Editor of National Advocate (New York).
1815–1819. Justice, Marine Court, New York City.
1816–1827. U. S. Supreme Court Reporter.
1821. Member, New York Constitutional Convention.
1823. Member, New York Assembly.
1827–1835. Chargé d'affaires, Copenhagen.

(Continued on next page)

He was at the farthest remove from being what Samuel Johnson thought Lord Coke was, a "mere lawyer." This appears not only in the events of his life, but in his writings, and was clearly illustrated when in April, 1842, he was elected a member of the Academy of Moral and Political Sciences in the French Institute. At that time it was debated whether he should be admitted into the History section or that of Jurisprudence, the latter finally being selected. The choice was undoubtedly correct, but there would have been nothing inappropriate in considering him a historian. All of his writings even on strictly legal subjects have a historical trend, and he had to his credit many periodical articles and several books on non-legal topics. In 1826, he had published in New York a book entitled "Some Account of the Life, Writings and Speeches of William Pinkney." A second edition was published in 1860 in the Library of American Biography, edited by Jared Sparks. While on diplomatic missions in Europe his researches in the history and literature of Scandinavia were recognized by his election, in 1830, to both the Scandinavian and Icelandic Literary Societies, and he continued his work in this field by writing, in Copenhagen, a History of the Northmen. It was published in 1831 both in London and in Philadelphia. Guillot, in 1844, translated it into French, and at the time of his death, Wheaton was engaged on a new edition of this work. According to his preface, it was his aim "to seize the principal points in the progress of society and manners in this remote

1835–1837. Chargé d'affaires, Berlin.

1837–1846. Envoy Extraordinary and Minister-Plenipotentiary, Berlin.

1848. Died, Dorchester, Mass.

period, which have been either entirely passed over or barely glanced at by the national historians of France and England but which throw a strong and clear light upon the affairs of Europe during the middle ages, and illustrate the formation of the great monarchies now constituting some of its leading states." Washington Irving, who reviewed the book,[3] said that throughout it, Wheaton evinced "the enthusiasm of an antiquarian, the liberality of a scholar, and the enlightened toleration of a citizen of the world." Among the earlier experiences of Wheaton's life were several which show that he was more than the proverbial technical lawyer. In 1806, he set up an office in Providence, Rhode Island, for the practice of law. This fact was announced by the following newspaper notice: "H. Wheaton informs the public that he has commenced the practice of his profession as an attorney and counselor at law—office over Watson and Glidding's store." He found time, however, to devote himself to public affairs, and wrote articles for the Rhode Island Patriot in support of Jefferson and Madison. At the age of twenty-four, he delivered a Fourth of July oration (1810), on the publication of which Jefferson was moved to say that he rejoiced over every publication in which such sentiments are expressed. "While these prevail all is safe." Perhaps on account of the judgment and ability thus shown, Wheaton was on his removal to New York City in 1812 appointed editor of the National Advocate, newly established organ of the Tammany Hall or Bucktail party, and afterwards edited by James Gordon Bennett. This post Wheaton held from December, 1812, to May, 1815, during the trying period of the war with England. Mr. Kellen

[3] North American Review, 35: 342–371, October, 1832.

(Appreciation, p. 15) says that he raised a new standard for contemporary newspapers, which had with a few exceptions sunk to the depths of scurrility and venality. At the end of the first year, he says, Wheaton "had made good the engagements of his prospectus, that 'this print . . . should never wound the feelings of virtue; never infringe the laws of decorum; and never spare the vices of political turpitude.'" According to Edward Everett, the liabilities and duties created by the war with England "were elucidated by him with the learning of an accomplished publicist and the zeal of a sincere patriot," and his paper was sometimes the vehicle of semiofficial expositions of national party policies. After his retirement from the editorship he continued his editorial contributions.[4]

Wheaton is not remembered as an eminent practising lawyer, merely because of his greater accomplishments in other fields. Although his schoolmate, John Whipple, said of him that while a law student he devoted little time to the technicalities of the law, and doubted whether "at any period of his life he could accurately state the difference between a plea in abatement and a special demurrer," having "too deep a keel for narrow rivers and shallow creeks;" yet Wheaton was constantly an associate of such men as Daniel Webster in practice before the United States Supreme Court.

He had also brief experience both as a judge and a legislator. At the age of thirty he was appointed (May, 1815) Justice of the Marine Court of New York City, in which capacity he served until July, 1819. In 1821, he was a member of the New York Constitutional Con-

[4] For an account of the National Advocate, see Hudson, Frederic. Journalism in the United States, pp. 282–288.

vention in which sat also Kent, Van Buren, Rufus King, Peter A. Jay, Erasmus Root and Chief Justice Ambrose Spencer. In 1823, he was elected to the New York Assembly in which he served one term, at the expiration of which he was an unsuccessful candidate for a seat in the United States Senate. His interest in national legislation had already been shown when in 1815 he framed a national bankruptcy law and advocated its passage by Congress. His mind was constructive in character, and therefore he was peculiarly fitted for a task to which he was called in 1825. The New York Constitution, which he had assisted in drafting in 1821, went into effect January 1, 1823. Some of its provisions made a revision of the laws necessary, and this was authorized by the Legislature, November 24, 1824. James Kent, Erasmus Root and Benjamin F. Butler were named as revisers. Kent declined the honor and John Duer was appointed in his stead. After his long years of undivided authority on the bench, Kent was averse to working with associates. "It would have been most convenient to me," he wrote to Butler, December 8, 1824, "to have had the duty of revising the laws assigned to me alone." It is perhaps fortunate that Kent declined, because he doubtless would have followed the model which he himself had helped to provide in the Kent and Radcliffe Revision of 1801. There would have been no attempt at rearrangement and consolidation, but merely the elimination of obsolete and repealed laws, and a re-enactment of the laws in force, in the order in which they had been passed. This would have been a far different result from that which the revisers actually accomplished, viz.: the elimination of the dead law, and the scientific simplification, correlation and development of the remaining living law.

Duer and Butler now prepared a plan which would not have been approved by Kent and with which Root was so unsympathetic that he retired from office. A new bill was then drawn up providing for the new style of revision and substituting Henry Wheaton for Root. It is presumed that the appointment of Wheaton was suggested by Duer and Butler. Wheaton had already acquired a national reputation for legal learning not only in the Common Law but in the Civil Law. In 1805, while in France, just after the accession of Napoleon Buonaparte, he had studied Civil Law at Poitiers, where he had translated into English the new Code. This, however, was never published because it was accidentally destroyed. There is a coincidence between this incident and the fate which overtook Edward Livingston's Louisiana Penal Code (See Chapter VII.). The new act including Wheaton among the revisers was passed April 21, 1825, and he served until March, 1827. Wheaton's connection with the actual work of the Revision of 1829 is best told in the words of William Allen Butler, grandson of one of the revisers, Benjamin F. Butler:[5] "In the correspondence of the revisers in my possession," he says, "there is no trace of any considerable work done by Mr. Wheaton in conjunction with his colleagues, although his name appears with theirs appended to the Revisers' reports to the Legislatures of 1826 and 1827. He prepared one or two of the earlier chapters, but, probably, besides this, did little more than to concur in the action of his associates. But, at the outset, he gave to their plan his hearty assent, and while no letters or memoranda by him are included in the papers of the revision, one

[5] The Revision and the Revisers. New York, 1889, pp. 18–20.

important document exists which, by a few words of endorsement in his unmistakable handwriting and phraseology, establishes the authorship and the date of the first written plan of the entire work. This paper of eleven pages of the coarse unruled foolscap of the time, is entitled "General Arrangement," and contains a sketch and outline of all that was afterwards embodied in the Revised Statutes, classifying the entire body of laws for the government of the State, under five leading heads. Prepared immediately after the passage of the Act of April 21, 1825, it brings into outline the work as it lay in the minds of the promoters of that act, and is a summary of the system they sought to establish. . . . This paper is endorsed, "Projet of General Plan of Revision handed in by Mr. Butler, May 11, 1825." It "submitted to the judgment of his colleagues what, probably, Mr. Wheaton alone of the New York lawyers of his day would have thought of designating a *projet,* a word which his habits of study as a civilian and a publicist suggested to him as best descriptive of such novel and far-reaching propositions. In this term, and in the marginal suggestions which he made, we find one of those incidental traits which reveal, by a casual touch, the individual character and distinct personality of the writer." His few words of endorsement "identify the earliest recorded effort at a written system of governmental statute law for an English-speaking people."

If Wheaton took no very active part in completing the revision of New York Laws, the reason is not far to seek. We have already seen that at this time he was engaged in practice before the United States Supreme Court, that he was active in politics, that he was a contributor to both the newspaper and periodical press, and that he had written a life of Pinkney. Just prior to this period he had published two legal works which were the result of exacting labor. The first was a Digest of the Decisions of the United States Supreme Court (New York, 1821); and the second was an edition of Selwyn's Nisi Prius (New York, 1823), into the text of which he inserted the principles extracted from 1,300 American cases. In a review of this book, Edward Everett said[6] that Wheaton had "fulfilled the duties of an editor in a manner which will detract nothing from his established reputation." All of this was done while he was also filling the important and, as he conducted it, laborious office of Reporter of the United States Supreme Court.

Wheaton's permanent fame rests on three great services performed by him in the capacity of law reporter, diplomat and writer on international law. To these, the remainder of this sketch will be devoted.

Wheaton's Reports

In our day, the office of law reporter of the decisions of courts has ceased to command that respect which in former times attached to it. It is no less honorable and important, but in the United States its duties have become so systematized and defined by statute that the work of the reporter is taken as a matter of course. Reporter succeeds reporter, with little notice from the lawyer, and none from the layman. But in Wheaton's time there still clung about the task some of the glamour which made Lord Coke willing to combine with the duties of Chief Justice those of law reporter.

[6] North American Review, 19: 155–158.

Wheaton served as United States Supreme Court Reporter from 1816 to 1827, and he had only two predecessors in the office, Dallas[7] and Cranch.[8] Neither of them held office by virtue of legislative appointment, the office itself not even being recognized by Congress. They received no salary and depended on the sale of their reports to recompense them for their investment. Financially it was a doubtful undertaking, for in 1828, eleven years after his ninth volume was published, Cranch wrote, "I have not yet been reimbursed the actual expense of publishing my three last volumes by $1,000." The publication of these three volumes was delayed until the years 1816 and 1817 because of financial difficulties, and therefore, when Wheaton took office in 1816, the cases decided from 1812 to 1815 were nowhere in print. "Mr. Wheaton," says Daniel Webster,[9] "commenced his labors as a reporter with no very flattering prospects, if we may judge by the demand for the volumes of his predecessor." The absence of demand was a matter of surprise to Webster because of the importance of the cases contained in the reports. "We should naturally suppose," he said, "that questions of such an interesting nature, would render the sale of these reports very rapid. Such, however, has not heretofore been the fact. The number of law libraries which contain a complete set of

[7] Alexander J. Dallas (1759–1817): Born in Jamaica, West Indies; studied law at the Inner Temple, London. Secretary of Pennsylvania, 1791; Secretary of the U. S. Treasury under Madison.

[8] William Cranch (1769–1855): Assistant Judge of the Circuit Court of the District of Columbia, 1801; Chief Justice, 1805–1855. In addition to his U. S. Supreme Court Reports, he published six volumes of Reports of Decisions of the Circuit Court of the District of Columbia, 1801–1814.

[9] Writings and Speeches, National ed., 15:44–54.

the Reports of Cases in the Supreme Court of the United States is comparatively small. A great portion of the profession do not ordinarily practise in the national courts, and many content themselves with buying other books which to them are indispensable. Yet the importance of the decisions must render the volumes necessary, as well to those who follow their professional labors elsewhere, as to those who are practitioners in the national courts. No gentleman can think he has a complete library while he has not the judgments of the highest judicial tribunal in the country."

Certainly, it was not from mercenary motives that Wheaton in 1816 proposed to take up the work where Cranch's unpublished manuscript ended. His plan, calling for a "regular annual publication of the decisions, with good type, and to be neatly printed," received approval, and he was appointed, without salary, by the Court. "As an inducement to undertake the task and attend the terms of the court," says Webster,[10] "the justices of the Court engaged to furnish him alone, and for his sole benefit, with all such writings and memoranda as they might make of their decisions, and which would aid him in reporting the cases." Accordingly for twelve years he made the business of reporting his chief employment, and while retaining his residence in New York went regularly to Washington for the duration of each term of court. He was the only person so employed, and the only one who received the assistance of the Court. After using the papers given him by the justices, he destroyed them. The importance of these details will

[10] Report of the copyright case of Wheaton v. Peters. New York, 1834, p. 6.

presently appear, and it is worth noticing also that both as advocate and reporter he had the confidence of the whole bench, headed by Chief Justice Marshall.[11]

The first volume of Wheaton's Reports was published in Philadelphia by Matthew Carey, who entered it for copyright in the office of the Clerk of the District Court of Pennsylvania on December 20, 1816. The sale of this volume was so small that Wheaton found it impossible to continue the work under the existing arrangement. He therefore applied to Congress for relief, which was granted by the Act of March 3, 1817 (3 St. at L. Ch. 63). This act recognized the right of the Supreme Court to appoint a reporter, and provided an annual salary of $1,000 to be paid on condition that he print and publish the decisions within six months after they were made, and that he deliver eighty copies of each volume to the Secretary of State for distribution to designated Government offices.[12] Before the publication of volume 2, in 1817, Carey had assigned his rights as publisher to Robert Donaldson, of New York, who published the rest of the series. The assignment gave him the right to publish of each subsequent volume an edition of from 1,000 to 1,500 copies. Under these conditions, during the twelve years of his service as reporter, Wheaton received as salary a total of $11,000, and in addition a share of the profits from the sale of the volumes. The latter could not have been large, although there was prospect of a growing and continuous sale. Four years after Wheat-

[11] The Associate Justices at the time of Wheaton's appointment were Bushrod Washington, William Johnson, Brockholst Livingston. Thomas Todd, Gabriel Duvall and Joseph Story.

[12] This act was continued in force by acts of May 15, 1820, and March 3, 1823. An act of February 22, 1827, provided that the volumes should be sold at "not exceeding $5" each.

on's retirement, Donaldson stated that the stock of Reports on hand unsold was worth from $25,000 to $30,000. To Donaldson and to Wheaton, therefore, there would have been a kind of irony in Charles Sumner's remark, in his obituary notice of Wheaton, that the Reports "embody what may be called the golden judgments of our national judicature, from the lips of Marshall, Livingston, Washington, Thompson and Story." [13] The characterization was, however, in the sense in which it was meant, entirely correct. In no period of our history have more important and far-reaching decisions been rendered by the United States Supreme Court than during that recorded by Wheaton. It was the Golden Age of the Supreme Court.[14] The right of the court to take jurisdiction in constitutional questions was upheld,[15] the doctrine of implied powers was developed,[16] and a limitation put on the powers of the states.[17] There were also numerous cases in maritime and international law arising out of the War of 1812.

The Reports of Wheaton are notable not only on account of the nature and importance of the decisions, but also because of the manner in which they are reported and the extensive supplementary material added by Wheaton. He "has not only recorded the decisions with accuracy," wrote Daniel Webster, reviewing the third volume,[18] "but has greatly added to the value of the

[13] Sumner: Works, 2:65.

[14] Carson: Supreme Court, p. 244.

[15] Martin v. Hunter's Lessee, 1 Wheaton, 304, and Cohens v. Virginia, 6 Wheaton, 264.

[16] M'Cullough v. Maryland, 4 Wheaton, 316, and Osborn v. Bank of the United States, 9 Wheaton, 738.

[17] Dartmouth College v. Woodward, 4 Wheaton, 518.

[18] Writings and Speeches, National ed. 15:44-54.

volume by the extent and excellence of his notes. In this particular his merits are in a great degree peculiar. No reporter in modern times . . . has inserted so much and so valuable matter of his own. These notes are not dry references to cases,—of no merit, but as they save the trouble of research,—but an enlightened adaptation to the case reported, of the principles and rules of other systems of jurisprudence, or a connected view of decisions on the principal points, after exhibiting the subject with great perspicuity and in a manner to be highly useful to the reader." This opinion is confirmed by an examination of all of the volumes. The appendices alone would make a closely printed volume of 508 pages. A considerable part of the appendices relates to prize law. "Whilst gleaning in the rich field of prize jurisprudence afforded by the late war," he says in the preface to the first volume, "it was thought expedient to subjoin a more ample view of the practice in prize causes than has yet been presented to the public, which may possibly serve as a check to those irregularites that had crept in, from the want of experience, in this branch of the administration of justice. Its doctrines have been developed by the court in a masterly manner; and we may contemplate with pride and satisfaction the structure which has been built up in so short a time, and under circumstances so unpropitious to the development of the true principles of public law." His notes to this volume, "On the practice in prize causes" and "On the rule of the War of 1756," were followed by notes on the same and related subjects in subsequent volumes.[19] There are extensive

[19] Vol. 2, Note 1. Additional note on the principles and practice in prize causes. Note 2. President's instructions to private armed vessels.

(Continued on next page)

notes also on the neutrality of the United States in the war between Spain and her colonies (vol. 4, note 2; vol. 5, note 5); on the slave trade, referring to the case of the Antelope (vol. 10, note 1); and on other matters not connected with maritime law—as patent laws (vol. 3, note 2), charitable bequests (vol. 4, note 1), and the Civil Law (vol. 5, note 2, and vol. 8, note 1). So conspicuous was his success as a reporter and associate counsel that as early as 1823, on the death of Justice Livingston, Wheaton was prominently brought forward to fill the vacancy. The appointment, however, went to Smith Thompson, Secretary of the Navy in President Monroe's cabinet. By 1827, Wheaton had acquitted himself well as editor, legislator, law reporter, lawyer and writer both in law and in general literature; unquestionably his star was in the ascendant, and there lay before him the prospect of both honor and profit. It was then that President J. Q. Adams offered him the diplomatic post of Chargé d'Affaires to Denmark. "Now came the parting of the ways," says Kellen (Appreciation, p. 19); "to stay at home meant certain ease in temporal matters, the sharing of professional rewards and successes, and a certain measure of local honor and usefulness; to go abroad meant large service to his country at small pay, but great friendships, perfect opportunities for study and growth, and ultimately, perhaps, the filling a unique niche in the World's greater Temple of Fame." He decided to go, relying on the small but apparently certain income from

Vol. 3, Note 1. Documents on the subject of blockades.

Vol. 5, Note 3. On the subject of prize law. Note 4. Act of March 3, 1819—Piracy.

Vol. 6, Notes 1–4. The case of the Amiable Isabella. Note 5. The case of the Bello Corrunes.

the sale of his twelve volumes of Reports to eke out a competence while in the foreign service of the United States. He arrived at Copenhagen on September 19, 1827. In less than a year he received the first intimation that his Reports might not only cease to be a source of income, but might be the cause of vexatious and expensive litigation.

Wheaton v. Peters

On Wheaton's resignation, the position of Supreme Court Reporter was filled by the appointment of Richard Peters,[20] of Philadelphia. He was reporter from 1828 to 1842, issuing sixteen regular volumes, and a seventeenth volume which contains nothing not in the first volume of Howard's Reports. If he had confined himself to the regular series of reports, he would have avoided many enmities, and would have spared Wheaton from financial loss. On the other hand, the enterprise on which he embarked, and the lawsuit which resulted, settled for all time in the United States the respective rights of the public and the reporters of decisions of courts.

In June, 1828, Peters sent out from Philadelphia a circular entitled "Proposals for publishing, by subscription, the cases decided in the Supreme Court of the United States, from its organization to the close of January term, 1827." The circular states that on account of the heavy expense of the original volumes, about $180, there are few copies in some parts of the country. There-

[20] Richard Peters (1780–1848). In addition to his two series of U. S. Supreme Court Reports, he published a Digest of Cases in the Supreme, Circuit and District Courts of the United States, and edited Chitty on Bills of Exchange, 1819, and Washington's Circuit Court Reports, 4 vols., 1826–1829.

fore, he planned to issue in six volumes, at a cost not to exceed $36, a set of books to be known as Peters' Condensed Reports, in which would be contained all of the decisions of the Supreme Court to be found in the four volumes of Dallas, the nine volumes of Cranch and the twelve volumes of Wheaton. His own regular series of reports, then just beginning, would continue the Condensed Reports. Thus he would have in his own hands a complete series of reports from the establishment of the Supreme Court to date. It is a curious example of special pleading that Peters, while justifying the issuance of the Condensed Reports to reduce the cost to lawyers, issued his regular series at the same price which Wheaton was charging. In the preface to Peters' first volume of the regular series, he says: "It is held obligatory on the reporter, under the provisions of the act of Congress . . . to stipulate with the publisher that the price per volume shall be $5." The statute did not require this. It put the price to the public at "not exceeding $5 a volume," and there was no legal impediment preventing Peters from fixing the price at less than $5. Before issuing his circular, Peters had carefully considered the legal rights of his predecessors in office to the contents of their respective volumes, and he attempted to answer in advance questions which would be raised by them. "It is not considered that the work now announced," the circular continued,[21] "will interfere with the interests of those gentlemen who have preceded the reporter in the station he has the honor to hold. Deeply as he is impressed with the absolute necessity of the work announced, he would exceedingly regret such an interfer-

[21] Report of the copyright case of Wheaton v. Peters. New York, James Van Norden, 1834, p. 9.

ence. Their volumes will always be standards for reference, and of the highest authority; and every member of the profession who has ability to purchase them, will own them. The legal rights of the proprietors of those most able and valuable works will be carefully respected. Nothing will be inserted in the contemplated publication but matters which are of public record, and which, from their very nature, cannot be the subject of literary property. The opinions of the court, which are public property, are referred to." The announcement ends with the prophecy that the proposed work will "increase the demand for the original reports, as their superior merits and accuracy will, by its means, become more generally known."

The publication of the circular produced immediate protest from Judge Cranch who, in a letter dated July 18, 1828, informed Peters that he must insist on his legal rights because he was still out of pocket $1,000 for the publication of his three last volumes. To this Peters replied (August 14, 1828) that he did not intend to invade Cranch's legal rights, but that since "the opinions of the court cannot be the subject of copyright, neither can the facts of the cases be the property of anyone," and therefore, he concludes, his work will not be obnoxious to the laws protecting literary property. A protest written by Donaldson, publisher of Wheaton's Reports, on September 25, 1828, was answered by transmitting copies of the above correspondence with Cranch. The seriousness of the situation appears from Donaldson's letter, in which he wrote: "I readily anticipate . . . that you will not issue such a work, the effect of which would be to me literally ruinous on a large amount of property I have vested in the work, which I have been endeavoring to accumulate from my labor and care of twelve years; likewise the injury that would be done to my absent friend, Henry Wheaton, Esquire, by such a publication, and the result of which would be to deprive him and his family of the pecuniary reward due to his professional labors of twelve years."

Nevertheless, Peters went ahead with the publication of the Condensed Reports, issuing volumes 1 and 2 in 1830, and volume 3 in February, 1831.[22] The edition was of 1,500 copies, and 900 were sold by subscription before the date of publication. Judge Cranch took no steps to ascertain his legal rights through judicial proceedings, but Donaldson took action as soon as volume 3, containing the cases from the first volume of Wheaton, was issued. His threats to prosecute Mr. Halstead, a bookseller of New York, if he sold the volume, produced a new circular from Peters in the form of a letter to his publisher, John Grigg, March 2, 1831,[23] in which he offered to "indemnify and save harmless from all costs and damages all who publish or sell the work." He reiterated his determination to proceed with publication and now added to his former statement that the judicial opinions were not susceptible of copyright, the new claim that "there does not exist a copyright, legally secured, to any one volume of Mr. Wheaton's Reports." He asserted that neither Wheaton nor his publishers had complied with the statutes for securing copyrights.

[22] Peter's Condensed Reports:
Vol. 1, Dallas, 2, 3, 4; Cranch, 1, 2, 3.
Vol. 2, Cranch, 4, 5, 6, 7.
Vol. 3, Cranch, 8, 9; Wheaton, 1.
Vol. 4, Wheaton, 2, 3, 4, 5.
Vol. 5, Wheaton, 6, 7, 8, 9.
Vol. 6, Wheaton, 10, 11, 12.

[23] Report of the copyright case of Wheaton v. Peters, pp. 9–12.

Peters derived considerable satisfaction by announcing in this same circular that on March 1, 1831, Congress by joint resolution had authorized the purchase of seventy copies of his Condensed Reports.

Under these circumstances, Donaldson, in May, 1831, filed a bill in equity praying an injunction to prevent the further printing, publication and sale of volume 3, Condensed Reports; asking for an accounting and payment of what might be due Wheaton; and for further relief. The injunction being granted, the defendants, in September, put in their answer, and moved to dissolve the injunction. After argument the court, being divided, denied the motion, and continued the cause until final hearing. It was heard in January, 1833, the title of the case being Wheaton and Donaldson v. Peters and Grigg (Federal Cases, No. 17,486). Justice Hopkinson held that Wheaton had not taken the steps necessary under the statutes, and that no Common-Law copyright existed in the United States. He, therefore, dissolved the injunction and dismissed the bill (January 9, 1833). An appeal to the United States Supreme Court was immediately entered.

Peters then proceeded with the publication of the Condensed Reports, and issued the sixth and last volume in January, 1834. The case on appeal came on for hearing in the January Term, 1834. On the bench were Chief Justice Marshall, and Justices Story, Duvall, McLean, Thompson and Baldwin. The attorneys for the complainants were Daniel Webster and Elijah Paine; and for the defendants, Thomas Sergeant and J. R. Ingersoll. Wheaton, having been granted leave of absence in the autumn of 1833, was in the United States, where he remained until August, 1834. The arena was prepared, all the principals were on hand, and now began a combat which taxed to the utmost the intellectual capacities and legal knowledge of the contestants. The case as reported by Peters (8 Peters, 591; 8 Law. ed. 1055), fills 108 pages, and in an appendix he reprinted the opinion given by Judge Hopkinson in the Circuit Court. In addition, he issued a report of the case in separate form, which he dedicated to Chief Justice Marshall.[24]

This is not the place to follow the intricacies of the argument or the varying opinions of the Judges. The case takes its place with the great English copyright cases which were fully discussed by Counsel and Court.[25] Wheaton and Donaldson asserted their right on two grounds (1) under the Common Law and (2) under the acts of Congress. The majority of the Court came to the conclusion that no right of copy exists under the Common Law in the United States. Justices Thompson and Baldwin dissented on this point. The Chief Justice and Justices Story, Duvall and McLean agreed that whatever rights the complainants possessed must have accrued under the acts of Congress, and since they were left in doubt, after an examination of the evidence, whether there had been a substantial compliance with every legal requisite, the case was remanded to the Circuit Court for a further trial, by a jury, of the issue of facts. With this conclusion Justices Thompson and Baldwin disagreed, but for different reasons. They both, however,

[24] Report of the copyright case of Wheaton v. Peters decided in the Supreme Court of the United States. With an appendix, containing the acts of Congress relating to copyright. New York, printed by James Van Norden, 1834. Large 8°. 176 p.

[25] Millar v. Taylor, 4 Burr. 2303; Donaldson v. Becket, 4 Burr. 2408; Roper v. Streater, Skinner's Report, 234.

believed that the decree of the court below should be reversed, the injunction made perpetual, and an accounting directed. It might appear that the decision of the majority still held out some hope for the complainants, provided they could show that they had a statutory claim to copyright; but this is not the fact, because the court was "unanimously of opinion, that no reporter has, or can have any copyright, in the written opinions delivered by this court; and that the judges thereof cannot confer on any reporter any such right." Thus was settled at once and for all time in the United States the question of literary property in the written opinions of courts. To Wheaton the decision was a serious financial blow; but he harbored no grievance against the bench which had felt obliged to deliver it. "I have seen my judges," he wrote on January 13, 1834.[26] "The old Chief Justice received me with fraternal frankness. What a green old age! I have also had the pleasure of meeting many old friends of the Bar with cordial greeting. They are one and all against Peters, crying out that his conduct has been shameful. But he bears it off with brazen impudence. . . . I don't envy him his feelings." Peters went ahead with the sale of his Condensed Reports, and, in order to protect his literary property in his notes, duly entered for copyright the volumes of the regular series of his Reports. There is justice in the fact that the Condensed Reports were ultimately superseded by Curtis' edition of the Reports, that Wheaton's original Reports stand to-day on the shelves of every important law library, and that the publishers of the modern reprint "The Lawyers' Edition" would be the first to do them honor.

[26] Kellen: Appreciation, pp. 27–28.

Wheaton as a Diplomat

We have seen that Wheaton abandoned the role of reporter for that of diplomat. His appointment to the post at Copenhagen was of importance because he was the first regular diplomatic representative sent there from the United States. His only predecessor was George W. Erving, who in 1811 had been sent on a special mission in reference to seizures and condemnations of American vessels under a Danish ordinance of 1810. It was Wheaton's first duty to carry to a conclusion the negotiations begun by Erving. Although the Danish government never admitted that it had been guilty of violation of American neutral rights, Wheaton secured a treaty, signed March 28, 1830, by which three quarters of a million of dollars were paid the United States for distribution to American claimants.[27] For eight years Wheaton was accredited to Denmark, and during these years he not only carried on the duties of his office with exceptional ability, but performed a far more important service by the sympathetic study and exposition of Scandinavian life as shown in literature and history. It was in this period that he published his History of the Northmen, as well as many periodical articles on the Danish language, literature and institutions.[28]

The United States had not been represented at the Court of Prussia since the mission of John Quincy Adams in 1797. In 1834, the Prussian Government expressed the wish that Mr. Wheaton be sent to Berlin,

[27] For Wheaton's discussion of the questions involved, see Lawrence's Wheaton, 2d anno. ed., pp. 858–870.

[28] *e. g.* Essay on Scandinavian Literature, *American Quarterly Review,* 3:481; The Danish Constitution, *Foreign Quarterly Review,* 11:128.

and this was finally done by President Jackson. Wheaton, as Chargé d'Affaires, arrived in Berlin in June, 1835. In 1837, he was promoted by President Van Buren to be Envoy Extraordinary and Minister Plenipotentiary. A specific duty of Wheaton's mission was the establishment of commercial relations with the states of the German Confederation as set up by the Congress of Vienna. It was the work of six years to create the sentiment, fix upon the terms, and get the mutual consent of the respective governments to the proposed treaty, which was finally signed on March 25, 1844. The negotiation of the treaty was recognized by European diplomats and by American statesmen, including President Tyler and Secretary of State Upshur, as a brilliant achievement. It was the crowning event of Wheaton's diplomatic career. The United States Senate did not, however, see fit to ratify the treaty; and defeated it by a strictly party vote. This was a serious blow to Wheaton. "The failure of the measure," says Lawrence,[29] "on which he had founded the expectations of a permanent fame, and which had engrossed so large a portion of his diplomatic career, occasioned feelings of mortification and disappointment which seriously affected the happiness of his few remaining years." This disappointment did not, however, prevent him from rounding out an extraordinarily honorable career which in some respects has never been surpassed in our diplomatic history. He served continuously under six successive Presidents, J. Q. Adams, Jackson, Van Buren, Harrison, Tyler and Polk, and for twenty years was abroad in the interest of the United States. When Polk took office in March, 1845, Wheaton was in his sixtieth year of age. Having adopted diplomacy as his

[29] Lawrence's Wheaton, 2d anno. ed., p. liv.

life work, and having weathered the storms of so many changes of administration at home, he looked forward to transfer to either Paris or London. President Polk, however, had other plans which did not include retention of Wheaton in the foreign service, and his resignation was therefore requested. He delivered his letter of recall to the King of Prussia, July 18, 1846, but did not return to the United States until the spring of 1847. The interim he spent in Paris and London. His enforced retirement was a source of great disappointment to him and to his associates in the diplomatic service. He must, however, have been gratified by the marked expression of appreciation which greeted his return. Public dinners were given him in New York and Philadelphia, and the City Council of Providence ordered his portrait painted to hang in the Common Council Chamber.[30] He was immediately offered the lectureship on Civil and International law at Harvard College, and began the preparation of his lectures. But his health failed rapidly and he was never able to take up the appointment. He died at Dorchester, Massachusetts, on March 11, 1848, in his sixty-third year, and was buried in the city of his birth, Providence, Rhode Island.

Wheaton as an Expounder of International Law

If Wheaton's diplomatic career began with a disappointment—the failure of his suit against Peters; if it was marred, midway, by the rejection of his treaty by the United States; if it ended by recall when promotion was expected: it was also the period of his life when he rose to eminence as a writer on the science and history

[30] The portrait is by Healy. It is reproduced in the picture accompanying this sketch, engraved by T. Johnson.

of international law. It was while stationed at Berlin that he published both his Elements of International Law and his History of the Law of Nations. The fame which he merited and received as soon as these works became known to the learned on both sides of the Atlantic suffered no detraction during his lifetime or after his death. He was immediately accepted as the chief modern expounder of the science of international law. This must have been a source of satisfaction so great as to outweigh all disappointments, and he must have become conscious that he had been shaped by the whole course of his life for this lasting achievement. Before beginning the practice of law, he had spent a year abroad in France and England, an experience which broadened his outlook upon legal problems and turned his mind to public affairs generally. Then, after six years of law practice in Providence, during which period he wrote and spoke effectively on national questions, he had undertaken the editorship of the National Advocate in New York. War with England had already been declared, and therefore his natural turn of mind toward international affairs received a stimulus which caused him to treat the questions raised by the war with a technical accuracy and a broad-gauge statesmanship unusual in newspaper publication. The whole question of neutral rights was at that time extensively discussed by him and the right of expatriation argued in answer to Gouverneur Morris. He first published the opinion of Judge Story affirming the illegality of trade under enemy's licenses. Immediately after the close of the war, he published (in 1815) his first systematic treatise on an international legal subject. This was a Digest of the Law of Maritime Captures and Prizes

(New York, R. McDermut and D. D. Arden). Of this work Judge Story wrote to Wheaton (December 13, 1815): "You have honorably discharged that duty which every man owes to his profession, and I am persuaded that your labors will ultimately obtain the rewards which learning and talents cannot fail to secure." Writing in 1848, Charles Sumner said (Works, 2:65): "No American contribution to jurisprudence so early as 1815 has received such marked commendation abroad. Kent and Story had not then produced those works which have secured to them their present freehold of European fame." "In point of learning and methodical arrangement," wrote James Reddie,[31] "it is very superior to any treatise on this department of the law which had previously appeared in the English language." The prestige which this work brought him doubtless was responsible for his employment as counsel in many of the maritime cases resulting from the war heard by the United States Supreme Court.

Another germ from which was generated his later works was an anniversary discourse delivered by him on December 28, 1820, before the New York Historical Society.[32] In it he gave a "rapid view of the history of the science of public or international law." The advanced stage to which his thought had progressed is shown by the following quotation in regard to the nature of international law itself: "It is a fundamental error," he says, "into which some speculative writers have fallen, to suppose that the law of nations is merely the law of nature applied to the conduct of independent nations and states.

[31] Researches, Historical and Critical, in Maritime International Law. Edinburgh, 1845, 2:299.

[32] New York Historical Society Collections, 1821, 3:281–320.

It may, indeed, have a remote foundation of this sort; but the immediate, visible basis on which the public law of Europe, and the nations which have sprung from the European stock, has been erected, are the customs, usages, and conventions observed by that portion of the human race in their intercourse with each other." The skill which Wheaton afterward showed in finding and using pertinent material was developed through experience as an editor of technical law books, as a compiler of digests, and as a codifier of statute law; but the most potent influence in his preparation for writing on international law was exerted upon him while he was Reporter of the United States Supreme Court. It has already been remarked that the extensive notes to his Reports deal largely with topics in international law. This may seem strange to those who think of Marshall's great decisions as dealing chiefly with constitutional law. The fact is that his decisions on international questions are almost as numerous and important. It was these to which Wheaton's mind naturally turned as subjects for elaboration. The extent to which Wheaton was indebted to these decisions was pointed out by John Basset Moore, in 1901, in his address on John Marshall.[33] "During the period of Marshall's judicial service," he says, "decisions were rendered by the Supreme Court in 195 cases involving questions of international law or in some way affecting international relations. In eighty of these cases the opinion of the court was delivered by Marshall. . . . As an evidence of the respect paid to his opinions by publicists, the fact may be pointed out that Wheaton, in the first edition of his Elements of International Law, makes 150 judicial citations, of which 105 are English and 45

[33] Political Science Quarterly, 16:405.

American, the latter being mostly Marshall's. In the last edition, he makes 214 similar citations, of which 135 are English and 79 American, the latter being largely Marshall's; and it is proper to add that one of the distinctive marks of his last edition is the extensive incorporation into his text of the words of Marshall's opinions." [34]

Wheaton's entrance into the diplomatic service was the beginning of the last stage of preparation for his destined task. A writer on international law must not only be academically learned, but freed from insularity, and made catholic, by contact with men and events. For this contact Wheaton was fitted by two fortunate characteristics, —an ability for making friends, and an unusual facility in acquiring foreign languages. He was thus able not only to read the literature of European countries, but to become intimately acquainted with the thought of their people through the medium of speech. Add to these qualities the desire to write, and the steadying influence of experience, and we see his equipment as well-nigh ideal.

In the ninth year after entering the foreign service, Wheaton published the first edition of his Elements of International Law. The preface is dated Berlin, January 1, 1836. Two editions were issued during this year, the first in London (B. Fellows. 2 v.) and the second in Philadelphia (Carey, Lea and Blanchard. 1 v.). To the principal text is prefixed a Sketch of the History of International Law, based upon and largely quoted from the address which he had delivered before the New York Historical Society in December, 1820. Setting out to

[34] *e. g.* Case of the *Exchange;* Marshall's words from 7 Cranch, 116, incorporated into Wheaton's text, Dana ed. pp. 154–162.

"compile an elementary work for the use of persons engaged in diplomatic and other forms of public life, rather than for mere technical lawyers," Wheaton couched his thought neither in polished literary nor in abstruse legal phraseology. Rather he sought accuracy and perspicuity through discriminating arrangement and simple statement. So well did he succeed that to-day his name is inscribed with the greatest of American legal writers. "In jurisprudence," writes Professor A. C. McLaughlin,[35] "Marshall and Kent and Story and Wheaton, by judicial opinion or by written text, laid the foundations of American public and private law, and ably performed a creative task such as rarely, if ever, before, fell to the lot of the jurist." A reviewer writing in 1837[36] said that while the Elements followed the general lines of continental writers, using the same accumulated material, Wheaton had infused "into the whole mass the liberal spirit that prevails in the institutions and administration of the government of his own country. It is this last characteristic," he said, "which renders the work particularly valuable." The same reviewer said also that, so far as he was informed, this is the "first work upon the principles of the law of nations that has appeared in the English language." If he meant a work confined to this subject alone, he was correct; but he ought not to have overlooked the publication in 1826, ten years before Wheaton's work, of the first volume of Kent's Commentaries on American Law, part one of which, 200 pages long, is entitled the Law of Nations.

The richly merited success of the Elements encouraged Wheaton to attempt another work scarcely less important.

[35] Cambridge History of American Literature, 2:71.
[36] North American Review, 44:16–29.

This was an expansion of the Sketch of the History of International Law, which he had prefixed to the Elements. The French Institute having offered a prize for the best essay on the question, "Quels sont les progrès qu' a fait le droit des gens en Europe depuis la Paix de Westphalie?" Wheaton entered the contest. The result was a work of 462 pages entitled "Histoire des progrès du droit des gens en Europe, depuis la Paix de Westphalie jusqu' au Congrès de Vienne, avec un precis historique du droit des gens européen avant la Paix de Westphalie." (Leipzig, Brockhaus, 1841.) Commenting on Wheaton's failure to receive the prize, Charles Sumner said (Works, 2:67): "It was bold and honorable in Mr. Wheaton to venture in a foreign tongue the discussion of so great a subject. . . . [His work] whether in French or English is commended by matter rather than manner. On this account he was at disadvantage before the polished French tribunal. His effort received what was called *mention honorable;* but the prize was awarded to a young Frenchman, whose production has never seen the light. An impartial public opinion has awarded our countryman another prize more than academic. The same work in English, much enlarged, is now an authority." The later edition to which reference is made was published in New York in 1845 (Gould, Banks and Co.) with the title "History of the Law of Nations in Europe and America, from the Earliest Times to the Treaty of Washington, 1842."

In the meantime, one other work on international law had come from Wheaton's pen. It was an "Enquiry into the validity of the British claim to a right of visitation and search of American vessels suspected to be engaged in the African slave trade." [37] All of this work brought him many academic honors, among which were the Degree of Doctor of Laws from both Hamilton and Harvard Colleges, an honor which had previously, in 1819, been bestowed on him by his Alma Mater, Brown University.

With his History of the Law of Nations before the public he now turned his attention to the correction and revision of the Elements. The preface to the third edition is dated Berlin, November, 1845. It was published in Philadelphia, by Lea and Blanchard, in 1846. From 375 pages it had now grown to 655. The Sketch of the History of International Law is eliminated and in lieu thereof constant reference is made to the larger work into which it had grown. The two are in fact companion volumes which ought to be read together. If one adds to these the cases referred to in the twelve volumes of Wheaton's Supreme Court Reports, one has an unrivalled collection of material for the study of international law as understood in 1846.

In the preface to this edition, the author says that he has endeavored "to justify the confidence with which he has been so long honored by his country in the different diplomatic missions confided to him, by availing himself of the peculiar opportunities, and the means of information thus afforded, for a closer examination of the different questions of public law which have occurred in the international intercourse of Europe and America since the publication of the first edition of the present work." One of the questions more fully discussed was the exemption of a foreign Minister's house and personal

[37] Philadelphia, Lea and Blanchard, 1842. 151 p. A new edition was published in London in 1858.

effects from local jurisdiction. The expanded treatment was the direct result of a personal experience which Wheaton had in Berlin. The proprietor of the house in which he lived claimed the right to detain his goods at the expiration of a lease, in order to secure the payment of damages alleged to be due on account of injuries done to the house during the contract. The Prussian Government decided that under its law the contract itself had taken the case outside of the international rule exempting a Minister's effects from process. The controversy was terminated, as between the parties, by the proprietor of the house restoring Wheaton's goods on payment of a reasonable compensation for the injuries done to the premises; but the principles involved were the subject of extensive correspondence between the Governments of Prussia and the United States.[38]

One other edition of the Elements was prepared by Wheaton. This was in the years 1846 and 1847, just after his recall from Berlin. It was written in French and published in Paris and Leipzig, by Brockhaus, in 1848. It is known as the fourth edition. The preface is dated, Paris, April 15, 1847. The sixth and seventh editions, edited by Lawrence, and the eighth, edited by Dana, will presently be commented upon. Of the so-called "English editions," there have been five, all published in London, the earliest appearing in 1878 and the latest in 1916. There was another series of French editions, as well as issues in Spanish and Chinese.[39] The

[38] See Wheaton, Elements, 3d ed., pp. 274–287.

[39] Wheaton, Elements of International Law:

"Regular" editions.

1st ed. 1836. London.
2d ed. 1836. Philadelphia.

(Continued on next page)

publication of this Chinese edition was, according to Mr. Dana,[40] an important event. "The most remarkable proof of the advance of Western civilization in the East is the adoption of this work of Mr. Wheaton, by the Chinese Government, as a textbook for its officials, in international law, and its translation into that language in 1864, under imperial auspices. The translation was made by the Rev. W. A. P. Martin, D. D., an American missionary, assisted by a commission of Chinese scholars appointed by Prince Kung, Minister of Foreign Affairs, at the suggestion of Mr. Burlingame, the United States Minister to whom the translation is dedicated."

Lawrence v. Dana

Henry Wheaton was not a litigious man; he went through life engrossed in work of a high order, free from vanity, dignified, peace-loving, mindful of the rights of his neighbors. That his Reports were the sub-

3d ed. 1846. Philadelphia.
4th ed. 1848. Leipzig and Paris.
5th ed. 1853. Leipzig and Paris.
6th ed. 1855. Boston (Lawrence).
7th ed. 1863. Boston (Lawrence).
8th ed. 1866. Boston (Dana).
9th ed. 1921. (In preparation).

"English" editions.

1st ed. 1878. London (Boyd).
2d ed. 1880. London (Boyd).
3d ed. 1889. London (Boyd).
4th ed. 1904. London (Atlay).
5th ed. 1916. London (Phillipson).

French editions.

1st ed. 1848. Leipzig and Paris. (Fourth "regular" ed.)
2d ed. 1853. Leipzig and Paris (Fifth "regular" ed.)
3d ed. 1858. Leipzig 2 vols.
4th ed. 1864. Leipzig 2 vols.

40 Dana's Wheaton, p. 22, note 8.

ject of a lawsuit in which he was obliged to participate must have been very distasteful to him. Yet his name will always be associated with the great copyright case of Wheaton v. Peters. It is a singular circumstance that the chief literary work of such a man should, years after his death, have been the occasion for an even greater copyright case, fought out with a persistence and rancor which embittered the lives of two men. These were William Beach Lawrence and Richard Henry Dana, both of them editors of Wheaton's Elements. The former, born in 1800, was a graduate of Columbia College, and for many years a prominent New York lawyer, being at one time a partner of Hamilton Fish. He had a varied career during which he held a diplomatic post at London, was Governor of Rhode Island, and a lecturer on international law at Columbia College. Dana, born in 1815 of a famous New England family, was a graduate of Harvard College and the Dane Law School. Everyone knows him as the author of "Two Years before the Mast." He practised law in Boston, was United States attorney for the Massachusetts district during the Civil War, and from 1866 to 1868 was a lecturer on international law at Harvard College.

When Wheaton died, he left a widow and three children. The family was in moderate circumstances, and therefore, after a few years, Mrs. Wheaton sought some means of increasing her income from the literary works of her late husband. With this end in view she asked the advice of Lawrence, an intimate friend of the family. It was at first suggested that a new edition of Wheaton's Reports be published, but this project was abandoned in favor of a reissue of the Elements of International Law, as affording more promise of profit. Accordingly, in

1853, Mrs. Wheaton requested Lawrence to prepare a new edition with notes, introductory remarks and a memoir of Wheaton. This he agreed to do on condition that his services should be rendered gratuitously. The edition appeared in 1855 (Boston, Little, Brown and Co.), the text being based on Wheaton's edition of 1846 with addition in the appropriate places of the new material included by him in the French edition of 1848. "Of the present edition," wrote Edward Everett in 1856,[41] "about a third part is from the pen of Mr. Lawrence, who has discharged the office of editor and commentator with signal fidelity, intelligence and success. . . . The work is made in his hands what its lamented author would have made it, had he lived to the present time." The edition was copyrighted in the name of Mrs. Wheaton and she received all of the profits from its sale.

When the Civil War broke out in 1861, a new interest was created in international law, and Mrs. Wheaton requested Lawrence to prepare a new edition. The result was a much enlarged work—1232 pages as against 924 pages for the sixth edition—including an extensive "notice of the author," and an appendix of 137 pages by Lawrence. The preface is dated February 11, 1863. This bulky volume is characterized by very long footnotes in fine print, and the citation of many foreign law books, documents and journals, as well as manuscripts in the archives of the State Department of the United States. Of it, Justice Nathan Clifford said in 1869 (4 Clifford, 71), "Such a comprehensive collection of authorities, explanations, and well-considered suggestions is nowhere, in the judgment of the court, to be found in our language, unless it be in the text and notes of the

[41] North American Review, 82:32.

author of the original work." It was and still is a work of tremendous value, and subsequent events should not be allowed to take from Lawrence the credit to which he is entitled. The edition sold out quickly, and Mrs. Wheaton, in whose name it was copyrighted, again received all of the profits. It was a high-minded act of friendship to her and a tribute to the memory of Wheaton that Lawrence refused any pecuniary benefits from his editorial labors. If he had an intense pride in his work, surely this was pardonable. Unfortunately, however, his thought did not stop there. He felt that his name had now become indissolubly connected with Wheaton's, and he said that his "position to Wheaton was as that of Coke to Littleton." No one dreamed of separating these classics, and so it would be inappropriate for anyone else during his lifetime to become an editor of the Elements. Anyone who controverted this opinion obviously could not retain his friendship. Therefore trouble developed during the preparation of the edition of 1863. The publishers had more than a business interest in the work, for Mr. Charles C. Little, senior member of Little, Brown and Company, was the husband of one of Wheaton's daughters. That the two men were at first on friendly terms appears from the fact that Lawrence made his home with the Littles in Cambridge, while the first part of the edition was in press. This relationship ended when Lawrence insisted that the title-page should bear the words "Lawrence's Wheaton," and "Second Annotated Edition." Mr. Little thought that Lawrence's name should merely appear as editor of the seventh edition. This was regarded by Lawrence as a "gross personal insult;" while Little thought Lawrence's demand a "most audacious piece of interference" with his rights as publisher. Lawrence won his point by the threat that he would abandon the unfinished edition, but all personal relations between the two men were at an end. As has been said, the edition appeared and was successfully marketed; but both editor and publisher were dissatisfied. Lawrence began to feel that his rights as editor were insecure. He had learned that Brockhaus in Leipzig had issued a French edition in 1858, including Lawrence's notes to the edition of 1855. Having arranged with Brockhaus that the latter would pay to Mrs. Wheaton an honorarium of 6,000 francs on condition that he might have the use of Lawrence's notes to the edition of 1863, Lawrence sought to obtain from Mrs. Wheaton an assignment of the copyright to both the original text and his own notes. This being refused, it was arranged by memorandum that "Mrs. Wheaton will agree formally to make no use of Mr. Lawrence's notes in a new edition without his written consent, and Mrs. Wheaton will give to Mr. Lawrence the right to make any use he wishes to of his own notes." This memorandum of June 14, 1863, was never ratified by any further document. Thus the Wheatons were left under the impression that no agreement had been made, while Lawrence relied on the memorandum to protect his interests.

So matters stood when, late in 1863, the question of a new edition was definitely taken up by the publishers. It then appeared that neither the Wheatons nor the publishers were satisfied with Lawrence's last edition. "This dissatisfaction," says Charles Francis Adams (Richard Henry Dana, 2:284) "was due to Mr. Lawrence's very prolix memoir of Mr. Wheaton prefixed to the treatise, rendering it unwieldy in size and costly in publication, while the notes and other matter which the editor insisted, as they alleged, on inserting, were unnecessarily long, and certain of them, it was further alleged, expressed the editor's personal views on current political events, more or less in avowed sympathy with the Southern rebellion. In the judgment of the publishers these facts seriously interfered with the sale of the work, and accordingly Mrs. Wheaton at last made up her mind to have a new edition prepared by another editor."

At first Charles Sumner was asked to undertake the work. After he declined, an appeal was made to Richard Henry Dana. Since 1861, the latter, as United States attorney for the district of Massachusetts, had been engaged in the trial of cases of prize brought into the port of Boston, and had on one occasion come into conflict with Lawrence on a point of law. He held no high opinion of Lawrence as an expert in international law. At first, he refused Mrs. Wheaton's request, but finally accepted the task, being "strongly drawn to it," he said, "from my interest in the subject, a desire to increase my knowledge of it, and, if it might be so, to add to my reputation; and I think I may truly say with an element of friendship for the family." It was distinctly understood between Mrs. Wheaton and Dana that none of Lawrence's notes should be used in the new edition.

Dana had been at work nearly two years, when Lawrence became aware of the fact. In January, 1866, he appeared in Dana's office in Boston and made a vehement and heated protest. As narrated by Dana,[42] there were no elements of pleasantry about the interview. Wall Street, New York, was pitted against Beacon Street, Boston, and there was no common viewpoint. When Dana

[42] Adams, C. F.: Richard Henry Dana, 2:297.

assured Lawrence that all of his original matter would be eliminated from the new edition, the latter replied that "he would see how that turned out when Dana's notes were published." In March, 1866, Mrs. Wheaton died, and in July following, Dana's edition was published. The preface did not contain anything tending to mollify Lawrence. On the contrary, it was so worded as to be sure to give offense to one in his state of mind. "This edition," wrote Dana, "contains nothing but the text of Mr. Wheaton, according to his last revision, his notes, and the original matter contributed by the editor. Mr. Wheaton's notes are indicated by letters. The original contributions of the editor are all in the form of notes, which are indicated by numbers, enclosed in brackets, and signed with the letter D." That is to say, he had done the impossible; he had separated Coke from Littleton. Not content with this statement, and to drive the point home, he went on to say, later in the preface, that "The notes of Mr. Lawrence do not form any part of this edition. It is confined, as has been said, to the text and notes of the author, and the notes of the present editor, who undertakes his work at the request of the widow of Mr. Wheaton, recently deceased, and of his only surviving children, his daughters."

It did not take Lawrence long to accept the challenge which he undoubtedly found in these words. At his home at Ochre Point, Newport, he began an exhaustive comparison of the notes in his own and Dana's edition. Later he permanently employed E. R. Potter, a lawyer of Kingston, Rhode Island, to continue, elaborate and codify the comparison. Almost immediately he found grounds for doubting the announcements made in Dana's preface, and he did not hesitate in speech, by letter and through the press to make sweeping charges of plagiarism and literary piracy. He also published his private correspondence with Mrs. Wheaton. Dana and the publishers took no public notice of these charges, relying on the copyright which Mrs. Wheaton undoubtedly held to the two editions by Lawrence, including both the original text and his annotations. But they were obliged to take heed when in October, 1866, legal proceedings were begun. A bill in equity was filed in the United States Circuit Court for the District of Massachusetts, "praying for an account, and for an injunction for the violation of an alleged copyright to a certain edition, with notes, of Wheaton's Elements of International Law." Potter's deposition, showing the results of his comparison of the notes, was taken in August, 1867. Dana's answer and Lawrence's reply were filed in the summer of 1868. The final response of Dana was presented in May, 1869. On September 20, 1869, the decree of the Court was rendered. The literature of the cause filled more than 1,000 printed pages, the result of three years' labor of the parties and their counsel.[43]

The case was of great popular interest not only on account of the questions involved and the publicity which preceded it, but also because of the prominence of the parties. We will pass over the technical questions of copyright which were exhaustively discussed, to point out that the case hinged on the question whether the memorandum of June 14, 1863, was valid and binding.

[43] B. R. Curtis and J. J. Storrow, for the complainant. S. Bartlett and T. K. Lothrop, for the respondent, Miss Wheaton. W. G. Russell, for Mr. Dana. Causten Browne for Little, Brown and Co. The full title of the case is "William B. Lawrence, Complainant, v. Richard H. Dana, Jr., Charles C. Little, Augustus Flagg, John Bartlett, Henry J. Miles, and Martha B. Wheaton, 4 Clifford, 1–88.

The court held that it was, and that although the copyright of the edition was in Mrs. Wheaton, her right to the use of Lawrence's notes was limited to the two editions of 1855 and 1863. The original gift of these notes, limited to these editions, and subject to a trust in favor of the donor, was emphasized and confirmed by the memorandum. This preliminary matter having been disposed of, the merits of the issue were discussed by the Court in answer to two questions:—First, "What use did the respondent who edited the edition in question make of the complainant's notes?" and second, "Was that use allowable, or was it of a character and to such an extent that it infringed the complainant's rights?" On these points a tremendous amount of evidence, argument and authority was before the Court. Dana had produced the entire manuscript, of 450 foolscap pages, from which his edition had been printed, and had described in detail the manner in which it had been prepared. Every note in the two editions in question had been dissected, analyzed, and compared by experts. All the great precedents in copyright cases had been cited by counsel and fully argued. The opinion of the Court was "that many of the notes presented in the edition edited by the respondent whose case is under consideration do infringe the corresponding notes in the two editions edited and annotated by the complainant, and that the respondent borrowed very largely the arrangement of the antecedent edition, as well as the mode in which the notes in that edition are combined and connected with the text." (4 Clifford, 83.) Since the Court could not of itself determine the extent of the infringement, it withheld the granting of an injunction against the sale of the Dana edition. Rules for determining the extent of the infringement were laid down and the cause referred to a Master in Chancery, Mr. Henry W. Paine of the Suffolk Bar, for examination and report.

So far, Lawrence was the victor. The decree justified his charge of unfair use of his notes, gratified the personal animus that he harbored against Dana, and confirmed him in the equitable ownership of the notes to his two annotated editions of Wheaton. But neither of the contestants was to have the satisfaction of a speedy conclusion of the case. Mr. Paine's indefensible delay in rendering his report doubtless operated much to the disadvantage of Dana; but it was also a denial of justice to Lawrence. The Master's first report was not filed until June 2, 1877, more than seven years after Judge Clifford's decree. Lawrence immediately filed objections, and it was subsequently excepted to by both parties. In July, 1879, the report was returned to Paine by direction of the Court for further proceedings, and they lasted until August of the same year. The final report of January 14, 1881, was a manuscript of 211 quarto pages.[44] According to Mr. Adams, "the report amounted to a complete vindication of Mr. Dana, inasmuch as the 146 instances of alleged gross plagiarism and servile copying had dwindled down to fourteen instances of technical infringement of copyright under the rules laid down in the opinion of Judge Clifford." The statement that the findings of the Master constituted a complete vindication is one on which opinions may differ; but, at any rate, after the filing of the Master's report, no further proceedings were taken in the case. "On November 25, 1893, the bill was dismissed without pre-

[44] For extracts from it, see Adams, C. F.: Richard Henry Dana, 2: 391–395.

judice and without costs pursuant to an order of court disposing of all cases in which no action had been taken for a long time." [45]

Whatever is the right view to take of the case, it was certainly disastrous to both parties. By it, Dana's reputation was seriously damaged and his health impaired. Having given up the practice of law, he went abroad in 1878, and later took up his residence in Rome, for the purpose, it is said, of writing a new work on international law to demonstrate his ability as an author. This work was never published, but extensive notes for it, now in the possession of his son, Richard Henry Dana, of Boston, were made. That they were of value is attested by Mr. T. J. Lawrence, who, in the preface to the first edition of his Principles of International Law (London, 1895), says that in the preparation of his book he had been helped "at every turn by the robust judgment and incisive arguments of Mr. R. H. Dana. . . . Mr. Dana had collected the materials for what I venture to think would have been the best of all books on international law, had he lived to write it."

On the other hand, Lawrence, although achieving what he conceived to be a personal victory, became obsessed with the idea of hounding his victim to the last. The spirit of the scholar in search of the truth was lost to him. His notes, concerning which he had fought so bitterly, were not used by him in any work in English; and although he published through Brockhaus a "Commentaire sur les éléments du droit et sur l'histoire des progrès du droit" of Wheaton (Leipzig, 1868–80, 4 v.), he never realized his ambition "of making a work that would be

[45] Letter from James S. Allen, Clerk, U. S. District Court, District of Massachusetts, April 5, 1921.

indispensable to cabinets as well as to judicial tribunals; a work which would embrace the results of the decisions of courts acting under the law of nations, as well as the diplomatic negotiations, on which depended the existing relations of the different states of the world." The futility of the whole controversy, as regards the two parties most interested, is shown by the facts that when the Master's report was made in January, 1881, both Lawrence's and Dana's editions had been sold out, that Lawrence died in March, 1881, and Dana in January, 1882.

One other ill effect has resulted from the Lawrence-Dana fiasco;—up to the present, no American editor and no American publisher have ventured on a new edition of Wheaton. Thus, without any fault on his part, his memory has not been perpetuated in his own country by the most effective and appropriate means. The long-deferred act of justice is, however, soon to be done. Professor George Grafton Wilson, of Harvard University, has in preparation a new edition of Dana's Wheaton, which is to be published in the series of Classics of International Law by the Carnegie Foundation.

In England, Wheaton early received recognition which continues to this day. In 1855, it was prescribed that candidates for promotion from unpaid to paid attachéships in the British foreign service should show that they possessed "such a knowledge of international law as can be acquired from Wheaton's Elements of International Law and Wheaton's History of International Law." This was "no mean requirement," says Heatley.[46] The acceptance of Wheaton's Elements as a standard work does not signify that there was no difference in foreign policy between England and the United States. Differ-

[46] Diplomacy and the study of international relations, p. 14.

ences of foreign policy have always existed; but, as pointed out by John Basset Moore, these differences did not come to the surface in Wheaton's work, since it was based largely on judicial decisions. As has already been noted, Dana's edition of 1866 was followed in 1878 by the first "English" edition. This was undertaken by the editor, Mr. A. C. Boyd, at the suggestion of the publishers, "there being no apparent probability of any new edition being brought out, either in England or America." Five English editions have now been published. Commenting on the last, issued as co-author by Coleman Phillipson in 1916, the Law Times said that "Wheaton stands too high for criticism." In the introduction, Sir Frederick Pollock says that Wheaton's merits "are, to begin with, those of a good scholarly lawyer of the first generation of American independence; but his combination of forensic, judicial and diplomatic experience gave him almost unique advantages in handling this subject."

APPENDIX

Bibliographical Suggestions

I. Cowell

Fuller, Thomas.
John Cowell.
(Fuller. History of the worthies of England. London, 1840. 1 : 420.)

Kennett, White.
Sketch of Cowell and his Interpreter.
(Cowell, John. Law Dictionary; or the Interpreter. London, 1727. Preface.)

Lee, S. L.
John Cowell, 1554–1611.
(Dictionary of national biography. 12 : 375–376.)

II. Littleton

Rigg, J. M.
Sir Thomas Littleton, 1422–1481.
(Dictionary of national biography. 33 : 373–376.)

Sir Thomas Littleton, 1402–1481.
(Law Times, 101 : 257–258, July 11, 1896.)

Sir Thomas Littleton.
(American Law School Review, 2 : 177–179.)

WAMBAUGH, EUGENE.

Biography [of Sir Thomas Littleton].

(Littleton's Tenures in English. Ed. by E. Wambaugh. Washington, 1903. pp. xi–lxvi.)

WAMBAUGH, EUGENE.

Bibliography of Littleton's Tenures.

(Littleton's Tenures in English. Ed. by E. Wambaugh. Washington, 1903. pp. lxvii–lxxxiv.)

Indicates the libraries which possess the various editions. The editions are listed in five groups, those (1) in Law French only, (2) in Law French and modern French, (3) in English only, (4) in both Law French and English, and (5) Coke upon Littleton.

WINTERS, WILLIAM H.

Bibliographical essay on the first printed book of English law, London, *circa* 1481.

(New York Law Institute Report, May 26, 1916, pp. 11–24.)

Refers to Littleton's Tenures.

III. Coke

ADAMS, FREDERIC.

My Lord Coke.

(New Jersey Law Journal, 19: 336–341, 356–364.)

BEER, THOMAS.

Coke literature.

(Ohio State Bar Association. Proceedings, 1909. 30: 182–206.)

CAMPBELL, JOHN, 1st baron.

Life of Sir Edward Coke.

(Campbell. Lives of the chief justices of England. 1: 245–357.)

THE CHARACTER OF COKE.
(Southern Law Review (N. S.), 1:107–122, April, 1875.)

CUSHING, CALEB.
Life and writings of Sir Edward Coke.
(North American Review, 13:255–286.)

D'ISRAELI, I.
Domestic history of Sir Edward Coke—Of Coke's style, and his conduct.
(D'Israeli. Curiosities of literature. 2d ser. London, J. Murray, 1823. 1:293–321.)

FOSS, EDWARD.
Edward Coke.
(Foss. Biographical dictionary of the judges of England. pp. 174–179.)

THE HISTORIC CASE OF COKE V. BACON.
(Green Bag, 9:516–520, November, 1897.)

HOPE, ANDREE.
Sir Edward Coke.
(Hope. Chronicles of an old inn. London, 1887. pp. 140–175.)

JOHNSON, CUTHBERT W.
The life of Sir Edward Coke, Lord Chief Justice of England in the reign of James I. With memoirs of his contemporaries. London, Henry Colburn, 1837.
8°. 2v.
Pages 404–485 of volume 2 contain a bibliography of Coke's works.

THE LIFE OF SIR EDWARD COKE, KNT.
(The Reports of Sir Edward Coke, Knt. in verse. 3d ed. London, 1826. pp. v–xx.)

MACDONELL, G. P.
Sir Edward Coke, 1552–1634.
(Dictionary of national biography. 11: 229–244.)

MANSON, EDWARD.
Striking figures in the legal history of England—Lord Coke.
(Law Times, 118: 109–111, December 3, 1904.)

ROSE, URIAH M.
Coke and Bacon; the conservative lawyer and the law reformer.
(American Law Review, 31: 1–17, January-February, 1897.)

SKETCHES OF EMINENT ENGLISH JUDGES—COKE.
(Albany Law Journal, 12: 276–279, October 30, 1875.)

WATT, FRANCIS.
Lord Coke as a person.
(Juridical Review, 27: 250–266.)

IV. Blackstone

CLITHEROW, JAMES.
Memoirs of Blackstone.
(Blackstone, Wm. Reports of cases. 1st ed. Preface.)

Clitherow was Blackstone's brother-in-law. The preface is dated, February 20, 1781.

DOUGLAS, D.

The biographical history of Sir William Blackstone, late one of the justices of both benches; a name, as celebrated at the Universities of Oxford and Cambridge, as in Westminster Hall. And a catalogue of all Sir William Blackstone's works, manuscripts, as well as printed. . . . By a Gentleman of Lincoln's Inn. London, Printed for the Author, 1782.

12°. 493 p.

FOSS, EDWARD.

William Blackstone.

(Foss. Biographical dictionary of the judges of England. pp. 97–99.)

MACDONELL, G. P.

Sir William Blackstone, 1723–1780.

(Dictionary of national biography. 5: 133–140.)

HAMMOND, WILLIAM G.

Bibliography of the Commentaries (of Blackstone to 1844.)

(Blackstone, William. Commentaries on the laws of England. Ed. by W. G. Hammond. San Francisco, Bancroft-Whitney Co., 1890. 1: xxi–xxvii.)

SOULE, CHARLES C.

Blackstone bibliography.

(Legal Bibliography, (N. S.), 15: 8–9, January, 1903.)

Subdivisions: (1) Genesis of Blackstone, (2) English editions, (3) Works founded on Blackstone, (4) English abridgments, (5) Comic Blackstones, (6) French editions, (7) Criticisms, (8) Miscellany, (9) American editions, (10) American abridgments.

V. Kent

COXE, MACGRANE.

Chancellor Kent at Yale, 1777–1781. A paper written for the Yale Law Journal. New York, Privately printed, 1909. 53 p.

CURTIS, WILLIAM J.

James Kent, the father of American jurisprudence. An address delivered before the Alabama State Bar Association at Montgomery, June 15, 1900. New York, Evening Post job printing house, 1900. 35 p.

DUER, JOHN.

A discourse on the life, character, and public services of James Kent, late chancellor of the state of New York. Delivered by request before the judiciary and bar of the city and state of New York, April 12, 1848. New York, D. Appleton and Company, 1848.
8°. 86 p.

ELLIOTT, CHARLES B.

An American chancellor.
(American Law Review, 37: 321–347, May—June, 1903.)

KENT, JAMES.

An American law student of a hundred years ago. [Letter from Kent to Thomas Washington, October 6, 1828.]
(American Law School Review, 2: 547–553, May—June, 1911.)

KENT, JAMES.
Autobiographical sketch of Chancellor Kent. (Southern Law Review, 1: 381–391, July, 1872; Virginia Law Register, 3: 563–571, December, 1897.)

KENT'S COMMENTARIES. [Review of volumes 1 and 2.] (Legaré, Hugh S. Writings. Charleston, 1845. 2: 102–141.)

KENT, WILLIAM.
Memoirs and letters of James Kent, LL.D., late chancellor of the state of New York. Author of "Commentaries on American law," etc. By his great-grandson, William Kent, of the New York bar. Boston, Little, Brown & Co., 1898.
8°. x, 341 p.

MARTIN, CHARLES S.
Chancellor James Kent.
(Green Bag, 7: 153–165, April, 1895.)

OBITUARY. JAMES KENT. Supreme Court, Tennessee, December term, 1847.
(Humphreys, W. H. Reports of cases in the Supreme Court of Tennessee. Nashville, 1849. v. 8 (v. 27, Tennessee Reports), p. ix–xix.)
Resolutions prepared by Thomas Washington, Edwin H. Ewing, R. J. Meigs, John J. White, and F. B. Fogg, and adopted by the Nashville bar, December 27, 1847.

SCOTT, JAMES BROWN.
James Kent, 1763–1847.
(Lewis, W. D. Great American lawyers. 2: 491–533.)

VI. Livingston

Blount, J. H.
The three great codifiers.
(Georgia Bar Association. Reports, 1895. p. 190.)

Gilpin, Henry D.
Biographical notice of Edward Livingston.
(American Law Magazine, 3: 1–16, April, 1844.)

Glenn, Thomas A.
Clermont and the Livingstons.
(Glenn. Some Colonial mansions; and those who lived in them. Philadelphia, 1897. 1: 297–331.)

Hunt, Carleton.
Edward Livingston and the law of Louisiana.
(Law Notes (N. Y.), 7: 88–90, August, 1903.)

Hunt, Charles H.
Life of Edward Livingston. New York, D. Appleton & Co., 1864.
8°. xxiv, 448 p.

Smith, Eugene.
Edward Livingston and the Louisiana codes.
(Columbia Law Review, 2: 24–36, January, 1902.)

A System of Penal Law for the State of Louisiana.
(North American Review, 43: 297–336, October, 1836.)

The Works of Edward Livingston.
(Law Magazine and Review (N. S.), 3: 332–344, April, 1874.)

VII. Wheaton

EVERETT, EDWARD.
Life, services and works of Henry Wheaton.
(North American Review, 82: 1–32.)

JONES, FRANCIS R.
Henry Wheaton.
(Green Bag, 16: 781–785, December, 1904.)

KELLEN, WILLIAM VAIL.
Henry Wheaton. An appreciation, being the address delivered before the alumni of Brown University on the occasion of the one hundredth anniversary of his graduation, June 17, 1902.
8°. 52 p.

LAWRENCE, WILLIAM BEACH.
Notice of the author [Wheaton] by the editor.
(Wheaton, Henry. Elements of International Law. Ed. by W. B. Lawrence. 2d anno. ed. London, 1863. p. xix-lxxvii.)

SCOTT, JAMES BROWN.
Henry Wheaton, 1785–1848.
(Lewis, W. D. Great American lawyers. 3: 243–285.)

SHEA, GEORGE.
Some thoughts on Henry Wheaton and the epoch to which he belonged.
(New York State Bar Association. Reports, 2: 95–103.)

SUMNER, CHARLES.
The late Henry Wheaton. Article in the Boston Daily Advertiser, March 16, 1848.
(Sumner. Works. Boston, 1870. 2: 63–73.)

INDEX

Printed in the United States
203625BV00003B/25-75/P